REMARKABLE
MOTOR
RACES

Pavilion

An imprint of HarperCollins*Publishers* Ltd
1 London Bridge Street, London SE1 9GF

www.harpercollins.co.uk

HarperCollins*Publishers*
Macken House, 39/40 Mayor Street Upper
Dublin 1 D01 C9W8, Ireland

10 9 8 7 6 5 4 3 2 1

First published in Great Britain by Pavilion, an
imprint of HarperCollins*Publishers* Ltd 2024

Copyright © 2024 HarperCollins

ISBN 978-0-00865969-1

This book contains FSC™ certified paper and other
controlled sources to ensure responsible forest
management.

For more information visit:
www.harpercollins.co.uk/green

Publishing and Design Director: Laura Russell
Commissioning Editor: Kiron Gill
Editor: Frank Hopkinson
Editorial Assistant: Shamar Gunning
Designer: Cara Rogers
Cover Design: Lily Wilson
Senior Production Controller: Louis Harvey

Printed and bound in China by RR Donnelley APS

Dedication

For Ella, who was taken far too soon,
and all you left behind.

Acknowledgements

I am especially grateful to Frank Hopkinson, who
first approached me to write this book, and whose
encouragement helped turn my initial scepticism
into a vision of what it could be. Thanks also to
the editors at Pavilion and HarperCollins for their
support and kindness throughout.

The book would not be what it is without the
input of the many racing drivers past and present
who kindly devoted their time to helping me realise
my aims. Primarily, I would like to thank Fernando
Alonso, Timo Bernhard, Sam Bird, Zak Brown, Karun
and Vicky Chandhok, Neil Crompton, Romain
Dumas, Jacky Ickx, Kevin Magnussen, Helmut
Marko, Daniel Ricciardo, Jim and Steve Richards,
Carlos Sainz, John Watson and Mark Webber.
But I owe a debt to all the racers over the years
who have given me the privilege of an insight into
the incredible thing they do. In addition, on the
officialdom side, COTA chairman Bobby Epstein
and Ryosuke Suzuki at Suzuka were generous with
their time and support.

And last but by no means least, Gil de Ferran,
whom I miss greatly, but who was a fount of
knowledge, wisdom, insight and joy for the 32 years
I had the privilege to know him.

PAGE 4: Team Nasser Racing's Qatari driver Nasser Al-Attiyah
and his French co-driver Mathieu Baumel navigating dunes
during Stage 6 of the Dakar Rally 2024, held in Saudi Arabia.

REMARKABLE
MOTOR
RACES

ANDREW BENSON

PAVILION

Contents

Introduction

What is a race track? In its simplest form, it is the venue for a motor race, in the same way that a football ground hosts a match. But a race track is so much more than that.

Football grounds have their own character and style – the Bernabéu is different from Old Trafford, is different from the San Siro. But the playing surfaces are defined, flat areas of grass with the same markings on them, the same size goals, wherever they are.

For Lionel Messi, the pitch is the place where he expresses his genius, but barring a few intricacies – is it wet or dry, for example? – the stage is the same everywhere he goes, even if the theatre and its ambience changes.

In football, and other sports played on a pitch or court, the opposition is the challenge. The pitch is a repeating platform on which to face it.

For a racing driver, though, each 'pitch' is different. The tracks might all be strips of asphalt – unless it's a rally, of course – but each one has its own design, its own length, its own sequence of corners, its own gradients and bumps and angles and cambers and kerbs.

Racing drivers face a test on multiple levels. They, too, have to beat their competition. But a large part of doing so involves being better at confronting the challenges of the circuit itself – and going faster around it than anyone else. And that requires the driver to fine-tune the behavior of the car to the demands of the circuit, via mechanical and aerodynamic changes, to give them the confidence to drive the car to the absolute limit of grip and performance. They then have to deliver that level of near perfection over and over again throughout the course of a race.

So race drivers and the places they compete are locked in a duality. The track is defined by the action – who won, driving what and how – but so, also, the action is defined by the track.

The circuit is the first-order challenge; you'll likely win if you can go around it faster than anyone else. The competition, while primary in terms of results, is almost secondary in terms of what the driver is facing. The driver might have to prove their superiority in a one-to-one battle, but that is unlikely to be won if the competitor does not master the circuit more completely than their rival.

A race track, then, does not just host a race. It defines it. Each circuit is different. Some are relatively simple; some are immensely complex. Some are short, some very long. Some are slow; some frighteningly fast. On some it's quite difficult to crash; others almost lure drivers into them.

RIGHT: Monaco is the epitome of Formula 1, and the Tabac/ Swimming Pool section around the harbour is one of the most spectacular places to watch racing cars in action.

BELOW: Former IndyCar driver and McLaren motorsport consultant Gil de Ferran (left) with Sauber's Alessandro Alunni Bravi on the grid in 2023. The irreplaceable De Ferran provided valuable insight into the US circuits for this book.

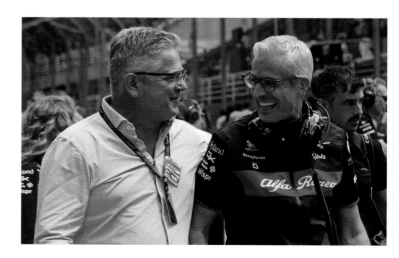

In a race at Monaco, you know there will be little if any overtaking; the claustrophobia of a street circuit in a seaside principality built on a Mediterranean cliff face is reflected in the character of the racing itself. At Spa-Francorchamps, where sweeping vistas of Belgium's forested valleys and hills form the backdrop to a race track on a grand scale, the openness of the setting is mirrored by the action on track. At Japan's Suzuka, jeopardy is always around the corner. In sand-blown Bahrain, a grand prix will be defined by tyre degradation. Abu Dhabi's Yas Marina, well, it may be one of the most boring spectacles of your life.

Is the ambient temperature going to be a factor, as in the tropical heat and oppressive humidity of Singapore, for example? Is the circuit dangerous, like the classic Nürburgring Nordschleife, or relatively safe, in the manner of the modern autodromes by German circuit designer Hermann Tilke.

Although that last question is one of degree, it comes with the understanding that no race circuit can ever be safe when the activity taking place on it involves human beings driving projectiles around at speeds of 320km/h (200mph) and beyond. This was proved at the 2020 Bahrain Grand Prix, when one of the most antiseptic of twenty-first century purpose-built tracks became a vision of hell when Romain Grosjean crashed his Haas, and it wedged between the barrier strands, suspended above the ground, and burst into flames.

This all points towards why a book about race tracks and venues, as this appears to be on a superficial level, is not really a book about race tracks at all. It's a book about what they mean, about the events that have taken place on them, about how those events have been shaped by the tracks and how the tracks have been shaped by events. And it's about the athletes who

achieved remarkable things, driving amazing cars, sometimes in the most incredible and demanding circumstances.

When I set out to write this book, I discovered that I couldn't tell the story of race tracks without also detailing the experience of the people whose heroics made the circuits famous. I wanted to get to the heart of the locations, and give a sense of the feelings created by racing, or watching racing, there, rather than produce a list of statistics about length and age and winners, although there's some of that here too.

The first person I thought of, following this realisation, was Gil de Ferran. Who better to unpick the mysteries and magic of the Indianapolis Motor Speedway than one of the most eloquent, insightful and emotionally intelligent men ever to win there? De Ferran, a friend since 1992, did not disappoint.

Tragically, he died, far too early at the age of 56, before this book was finished. In one of the last conversations we had, I told him he was the centrepiece of the chapter on IndyCar. He seemed genuinely pleased and surprised – he was a humble as well as a brilliant man – and it's a great sadness that he did not live to see the finished article. De Ferran loved motorsport and I like to think he'd have liked this book as a result.

OPPOSITE: Daniel Ricciardo drives Helmut Marko's Alfa Romeo 33 TT3 in a Red Bull recreation of their motorsport director's astonishing performance in the 1972 Targa Florio.

BOTTOM LEFT: Former Brabham, Surtees, Penske and McLaren driver John Watson, photographed in 1982, while partnered for the second time with Niki Lauda at McLaren-Ford.

BELOW: Romain Dumas powers his way up Colorado's Pikes Peak in the all-electric Volkswagen ID.R.

I am eternally indebted to the drivers who agreed to speak to me and shared their insights. The brilliant Fernando Alonso explaining the 'rhythm of the night' for his graveyard shift at Le Mans, John Watson revealing the real story behind how the Nürburgring was taken off the F1 calendar, and sharing the harrowing and emotional testimony of Niki Lauda's near-fatal accident there in 1976.

Romain Dumas laughing nervously as he described the drop off the mountain awaiting anyone who makes a mistake at Pikes Peak in Colorado: "You would fall for a long time. It depends which corner, but you don't want to see which one. You don't want to look, but you know that it is very dangerous."

Timo Bernhard recalling the moment of realisation after Porsche tasked him with breaking the Nürburgring Nordschleife lap record in their 919 Evo. "On my way home from Weissach, from Porsche," Bernhard said, "I was like, 'Okay, (sharp intake of breath) it's going to be very fast. It's not a walk in the park.' I understood the dimension of it, speed-wise and everything."

Or, in one of the more candid revelations, Helmut Marko describing an encounter with a mafia chief after setting the lap record at the 1972 Targa Florio. And Jim and Steve Richards's memories of Bathurst – where between them they have won 12 times – created what is probably one of my favourite chapters (see page 52).

Jacky Ickx, who has won Le Mans six times, eight grand prix victories, the Dakar Rally and the Bathurst 1000 – making him one of motorsport's great all-rounders – made an important point, too, about the people who make it possible for these events to happen.

"Racing exists because you have fans and passionate people," Ickx said. "Drivers are the tip of the iceberg. The driver picks up the glory, or sometimes has to bear on his shoulders the disaster, but 90% of the result is made by the people you never see. They do it with no limit and with passion and total humility, but they live in the shade and don't receive the return the drivers do. The drivers are the reflection of those people."

The world is full of amazing races and race tracks, as well as a few humdrum ones. More could have been featured in this book.

The idea was to paint as broad a picture of the rich tapestry of motorsport as possible, to capture the history of the sport in broad strokes, and the essence of the places included. And perhaps even to whet readers' appetites to experience them themselves. For a motor race watched live

– especially a grand prix – is a whole different experience than one viewed on the television. The speed is much more apparent, the encounter much more visceral. And you'll be that much closer to what the drivers in the following pages describe.

OPPOSITE TOP: Jacky Ickx has had an amazingly varied motorsport career. Here he lines up on the front row of the 1971 Spanish Grand Prix while a policeman tries to clear his mechanic from the grid. Ferrari technical director Mauro Forghieri is on the far left.

OPPOSITE BOTTOM: Timo Bernhard photographed during Porsche's attempt to break the Nürburgring Nordschleife's lap record with the all-conquering Porsche 919.

ABOVE: One of the single biggest causes of accidents at Le Mans is the disparity of the racing machinery. Fernando Alonso explains why he took on an extra-long stint in the 24-hour race through the night hours.

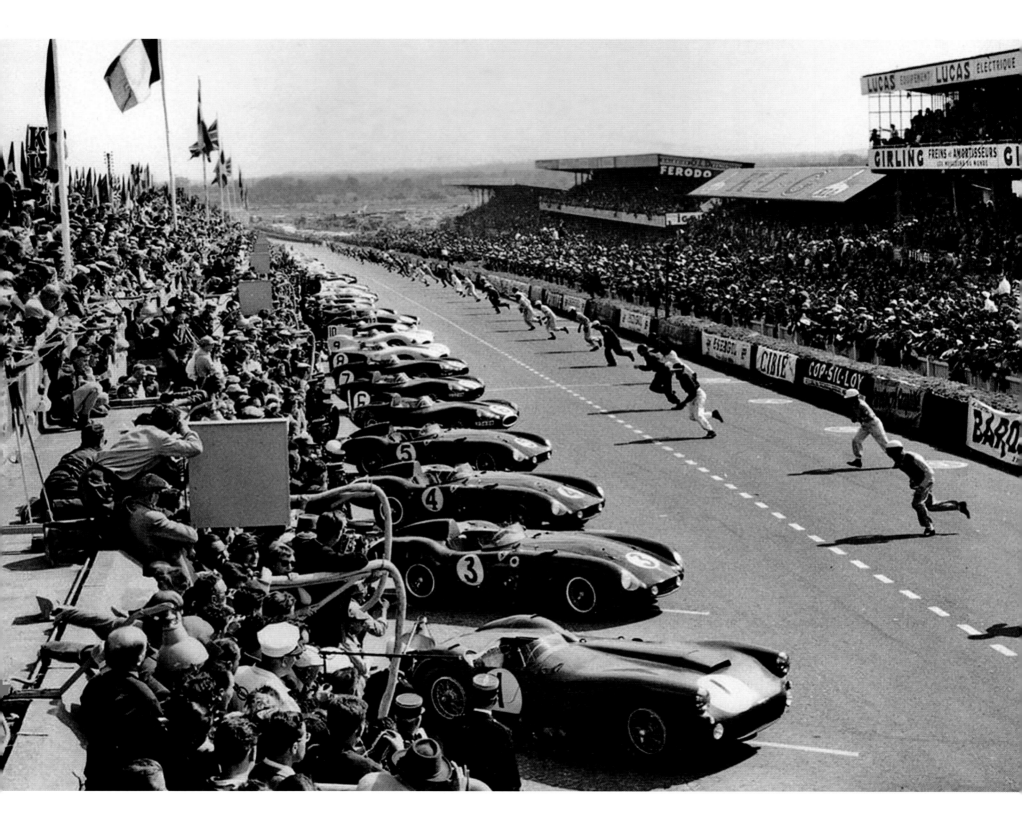

24 Heures du Mans

Le Mans, France

Les 24 Heures du Mans, often referred to simply as 'Le Mans', is a race that stands apart. It is not the only 24-hour endurance race, and it's not the only event that has celebrated a century since its inception, but it is unique in its history and its challenge.

For Fernando Alonso, who stepped aside from Formula 1 for two years to pursue his dream of

STEVE McQUEEN in
LE MANS
with ELGA ANDERSEN

directed by HARRY KLEINER · music by MICHEL LEGRAND
produced by ROBERT E. RELYEA · directed by JACK N. REDDISH
executive producer LEE H. KATZIN · a SOLAR production

LES 24 HEURES du LE MANS

PANAVISION · COLORE DELUXE · A CINEMA CENTER FILMS PRESENTATION

victory in one of the three most famous races in the world and achieved it twice, Le Mans is simply "magic".

History pervades at Le Mans – a race that can claim to be part of the very origins of motorsport. The town in the Sarthe region in the north-west of France was the location of the very first race to be given the title 'Grand Prix' – when Georges Durand organised the Grand Prix de l'Automobile Club de France in 1906.

And it was Durand again, in a meeting at the 1922 Paris Automobile Salon with Emile Coquille, the French agent for a British wheel manufacturing company, and Charles Faroux, the editor of the weekly magazine *La Vie Automobile*, who proposed the idea of a round-the-clock race for an entire day in the same area.

This was, as Richard Williams wrote in his exhaustive biography of the Le Mans 24 Hours, an example of, "a particular French genius for turning sport into mass spectacle", as evidenced also by the modern Olympic Games, the Tour de France, and the football World Cup.

Like those other grand events, Le Mans has generated its own legacy, permeating the consciousness of a worldwide audience like few others can manage. It has created enduring images for road-car brands; Bentley's modern

status is to a large degree the product of the British marque's five wins at Le Mans between 1924 and 1930, including four in a row from 1927, and the antics of the wealthy 'Bentley Boys', who drove the cars, and were famed for their joie de vivre.

Porsche also has the famous race to thank for its prestige. Would it hold such a status among the multiplicity of companies building high-end, road-going sports cars if it was not also the most successful manufacturer in the history of Le Mans? Would its cars even be as good without the racing heritage imbued in the company?

The original vision for the race was to encourage manufacturers to focus on building fuel-efficient, sporty and reliable cars, and the rules were devised to that end. The first race was held in 1923, and the format was initially envisaged as a three-year event, with the winner being the car which could go the furthest distance over three consecutive 24-hour races. But this idea was abandoned in 1928 in favour of a *'coupe de*

OPPOSITE: The typical Le Mans start at which Stirling Moss was a fine exponent. However this edition, the 1955 race, would prove a watershed moment in motorsport.

LEFT: Steve McQueen regretted not taking the lead in John Frankenheimer's *Grand Prix*, so produced his own motorsport movie which captured the essence of early 1970s Le Mans.

distance' – the winner was the car that could go furthest over a single full day – and that's the way it stayed.

The first iteration of the track headed into the town of Le Mans before turning south down the main road towards the village of Mulsanne, then turning right towards Arnage and finally back towards the town.

But in 1932, in the interests of safety, the town itself was cut out, and the track directed right from the pit straight to join the famous Mulsanne Straight at a fast right-hander named Tertre Rouge. The layout of just over 13km (8 miles) has remained fundamentally the same to this day.

There have been only two major changes since 1932. One was the bypassing in 1972 of the dangerous kink of Maison Blanche on the final run back towards the pits. It was replaced by the Porsche Curves, which are still incredibly high speed and challenging. Two chicanes were added to the 4.8km (3 mile) length of the Mulsanne Straight (officially known as the Ligne Droite des Hunaudières) when motorsports' governing body the FIA said in 1990 that it would no longer sanction a straight longer than 2km (1.3 miles).

It's the living, tangible connection between past and present that gives Le Mans its special appeal, along with a track that combines normal roads – with a crown and depressions caused by countless lorries – with the smoother style of a closed circuit. Two-time winner Timo Bernhard says: "Le Mans is from a completely different era.

TOP: Unknowingy, Dan Gurney, winner with AJ Foyt in 1967, has just started a motorsport tradition by spraying his first winner's bottle of champagne on the crowd (now placed on the floor while a less-than-pleased commissaire presents the laurels).

RIGHT: The Ferrari vs Ford battle swung decisively the way of the GT40 in 1966. Here, the No.2 GT40 of eventual winners Bruce McLaren and Chris Amon passes the Ferrari 365 P2 of Richard Attwood and David Piper.

"The part from the start-finish to Tertre Rouge is very close to being like a modern race track. Then you have Hunaudières until the Porsche corners, the whole back end of the track, which every day has multiple cars on it and you feel that from the asphalt. The movements of the car are completely different because instead of being completely flat, the car is tracking, moving.

Then the final part is mostly high-speed long straights and chicanes and high-speed braking. This is a completely different characteristic again."

Back in the day, it was normal to combine open roads with a shorter or longer part of closed race track. Le Mans is probably one of the last, or maybe the last, race track that still has that.

The history of Le Mans, whether it was in the era of modified road cars through to the 1950s, or the emergence of prototypes from the 1960s, tends to fall into periods of domination by

BELOW: The yellow Ford GT40 Mk IV of Bruce McLaren and Mark Donohue finished 4th in 1967, 29 laps behind the sister car of Dan Gurney and AJ Foyt.

specific marques. Technology moves on and one company steals a march on the rest.

As Bentley were the predominant marque in the 1920s, so Alfa Romeo forged its reputation with four consecutive wins for its celebrated 8C from 1931–34. Jaguar predominated in the 1950s, with five wins amid a powerful rivalry with Ferrari, whose victories in 1954 and 1958 were the precursors to their six consecutive wins at the start of the 1960s. That led to the famous Ford vs Ferrari battles of the late 1960s, with Ford's famous GT40 taking over from their Italian rivals with four straight wins from 1966–69.

Porsche then dominated the late 1970s and 1980s, as well as winning four times in the 1990s, before Audi won 13 times in 15 years from 2000, during which period Dane Tom Kristensen won eight of his record-breaking nine victories, including six in a row from 2000–2005. After another three wins for Porsche in the mid-2010s, Toyota has become the predominant manufacturer in recent years.

Behind the list of winners is a multitude of stories that tell of the history of motorsport. Jaguar's 1955 victory may well have gone the way of Mercedes, who had Juan Manuel Fangio and

Stirling Moss, the preeminent drivers of the era sharing a 300SL, had the race not been hit by the sport's most devastating ever disaster. Just over a couple of hours into the race, Pierre Levegh's Mercedes was launched into the crowd on the pit straight following a mix-up between Mike Hawthorn's Jaguar and the Austin Healey of Lance Macklin. Hawthorn, who had just passed Macklin, braked suddenly in front of him after receiving the order to pit. Macklin swerved to avoid the Jaguar, into the path of Levegh, whose car took off and cartwheeled down the track, bursting into flames.

The engine, radiator and gearbox smashed through the crowd for 100 metres (330 ft). The bonnet came off and decapitated people. Levegh was killed instantly, his skull smashed after being thrown from the car and landing on the track. The car, made of magnesium alloy, burned fiercely for hours. In total, 84 people were killed and many more injured. Mercedes withdrew from the race in the middle of the night – Jaguar rejecting their offer to do likewise – and, after completing the rest of the season, the German manufacturer would not return to top-level motorsport for another 34 years.

The disaster led to changes to the Sarthe circuit, especially around the pits, where the kink that meant Levegh's car was always heading towards the crowd was straightened out and the straight widened, to give room for a deceleration lane.

That was not the only time in Le Mans' 100 years that tragedy led to changes. Traditionally, Le Mans started with the cars lined up against the pit wall and the drivers on the other side of the track. When the signal was given, the drivers would sprint across the track, jump into the cars, start their engines and get on their way. But in 1969 the safety campaign that was gaining momentum in F1 through Jackie Stewart came to Le Mans. Ickx, like Stewart, one of the leading grand prix drivers of the era, was racing in a Ford GT40. He decided that the traditional start was too dangerous. In their haste not to lose position, drivers were too often heading into the race with their seat belts either undone or only partially fastened. Ickx refused to be a part of it, deciding instead to walk across the track and

OPPOSITE: Cars head down the main straight during the 100th anniversary running of *Les 24 Heures du Mans* in 2023.

ABOVE RIGHT: All-time Le Mans great, Tom Kristensen clinched his ninth and final win in 2013 driving an Audi R18 e-tron.

RIGHT: Fernando Alonso practises a driver change with his Toyota Gazoo Racing TS050 hybrid car in 2018.

take his time to fasten his belts before getting under way... and was almost collected by a car as he did so. What happened next changed Le Mans forever.

"To put on a six-point belt at 300km/h (186mph) with one hand," Ickx recalls, "honestly it is an exercise in which I was never successful. I tried, but it's impossible. And I really doubted jumping in a car and going 330km/h, you don't care about your seat belt or whatever. Then, boom, you race.

"There were still a few people in those days saying, 'Oh, it's better to be ejected from a car than staying in.' But clearly already a seat belt was a must. So I decided to take my time and start eventually last instead of running to it. And then the rest of the story is the guy who started last and finished first."

In one of the most extraordinary races in Le Mans history, Ickx and co-driver Jackie Oliver beat the Porsche 908 of Gérard Larrousse and Hans Herrmann by just 120 metres (394 ft), despite dropping to the back due to Ickx's start.

Ickx adds: "People often said to me: 'You have changed the Le Mans start.' It is a lovely story but it's not true. It was an inspiration, for sure, but I just had the feeling it was not a really good idea to start without seatbelts.

"The man who changed Le Mans was John Woolfe driving a private Porsche 917. The car was not so easy to drive. He lost it at Maison Blanche in a very tragic and awful accident on lap one, and killed himself without a seat belt."

TOP: The No.50 Ferrari 499P of Antonio Fuoco, Miguel Molina, and Nicklas Nielsen had taken pole in qualifying, but finished the 2023 race in fifth.

LEFT: Peugeot's aggressive-looking 9X8 finished the centenary race back in eighth place, but only 12 laps behind.

The character of Le Mans has changed in other ways since then, too. Traditionally, it was a race in which drivers had to nurse their cars to the finish. In the modern era, with increased reliability, that is not really the case. As Ickx puts it: "It was an endurance race. Literally. Today it is a grand prix. Because you know your car can make it. It's flat out."

An example of that change came with Alonso's first win, alongside Sébastien Buemi and Kazuki Nakajima, for Toyota in 2018. Their car had dropped more than two minutes behind the sister Toyota after problems in the first hours of the race, but that all changed with a remarkable quadruple stint from Alonso in the middle of the night.

He made up all the lost time in an identical car and clawed right back on to the tail of the other Toyota, from where he handed over to Nakajima, who retook the lead and the team went on to victory. Towards the end of that stint, Alonso had gone on to the radio and said he was happy to continue for longer if they wanted because he had "found the rhythm of the night".

Alonso told me for this book: "The night stint probably changed the outcome of my first Le Mans. It was just an extra risk in terms of overtaking cars. I entered in a very focused state of mind, in a mood that I was seeing just the track and the lapped cars.

"I tried to identify from the lights which car it was – GT, LMP2 or LMP1 – and thanks to that, just programme the next overtaking on that lapped car, using the (hybrid) energy in a different way.

"To keep the rhythm of the night high helped the tyre temperature a lot. So, the slower you go at one point, the less grip you have, because the tyres get too cold. So if you met traffic in a wrong place and spent three or four corners behind GTs or something, that puts the

tyres not in a perfect window. So this level of concentration and optimising the lapped cars kept the tyres in a very nice window and I felt unstoppable at that time."

It's a nice summation of the challenge of Le Mans – 24 hours non-stop racing, negotiating day and night, changing temperatures and weather conditions, against several different categories of cars, with dramatically varying performance, some piloted by amateurs, little more than weekend racers, others by the absolute elite.

"On the warm-up lap and the lap to grid," Bernhard says, "you feel all the crowd is there and there is no space from start to finish all

around the lap, basically it is just crowded with people. You feel this immense tradition and history, this passion for racing. It is just a huge race. Not only inside motor racing; inside sport. It is one of the big events on earth, plus the dimension of 100 years. That's what you feel in the car."

BELOW: The big news for 2023 was the return of Ferrari to the hypercar category and Team AF Corse winning with their 499P. The consistency of finishers was striking, with 20 cars finishing within 20 laps of the winner. In 1966 it was three.

Acropolis Rally

Lamia, Greece

Greece's Acropolis Rally is known as the ultimate car breaker. Held on rough and twisty mountain stages, coupled with blistering heat and often choking dust, it has long been considered one of the toughest events in the world rally championship. The stages are notorious for uneven surfaces and rocks – sometimes quite large – which, at the least, are likely to cause punctures, and, at the worst, break a wheel or suspension and quite often caused retirement.

Inaugurated in 1951, the Acropolis Rally was a permanent presence on the world championship schedule – from its inception in 1973 until 2018 – and after a three-year absence, it returned to the calendar in 2021 with help from the Greek government, who saw it as a way of promoting tourism.

In its heyday the rally was held all over Greece, from Mount Olympus in the north, through central Greece and even down into the Peloponnese peninsula to the south. But the traditional start was always at the foot of the Acropolis in Athens. Along with the Monte Carlo, the 1,000 Lakes and the Tour de Corse, it was one of the centrepieces of the World Rally Championship (WRC) calendar.

As rallies became more consolidated in range, the Acropolis increasingly became focused on the area around the town of Lamia, and the well-liked stages in the Parnassus and Giona mountains to the south.

Ironically, perhaps, given the rally's reputation as a car breaker, the most successful driver in Acropolis history is the late Colin McRae. The popular Scot, killed with his son in a helicopter crash near his home in Lanark, Scotland in 2007, won a total of six times for the Subaru and Ford teams between 1996 and 2002. Why ironically? McRae's reputation was as an incredibly fast but often wild driver, who was prone to errors because of his tendency to push the limits.

Four drivers are tied on three wins each. And, as if to underline the rally's status, they are quite some names – two-time world champions Walter Röhrl, Carlos Sainz and Miki Biasion, and nine-time champion Sébastian Loeb, the most successful rally driver of all time.

The heart of the Acropolis was a stage called 'Tarzan', after the nickname of a former Athens policeman called Giorgos Burgos. He was diagnosed with tuberculosis in his early forties and moved back to his home town of Fourna to benefit from the fresh mountain air. His hut, at the Fourna area's Zaharaki location, became a resting point for rally crews. Despite speaking only Greek, Burgos entertained guests with a variety of local food and drink and was a much-loved character who died at 92.

In its original form, the 30km (18.5 miles) Tarzan stage was fiendishly difficult. Drivers would finish the section covered in dust and with streaks of sweat on their faces, gasping for a drink.

It slipped off the Acropolis route for a while after 1995 but reappeared in a shortened 20km (12 mile) form in 2003. It disappeared for a while again before being reconstituted in shortened but still challenging form when the rally returned to the WRC in 2021, its status underlined by making it the so-called 'power stage'.

TOP: Hamza Anwar ignores the 'don't cut' pace note and rolls his Ford Fiesta Rally 3 on the 2023 Acropolis. He was righted in seconds by spectators and on his way.

ABOVE: Unusually, the 2023 Acropolis Rally experienced high rainfall creating spectacular fords along sections of the route.

OPPOSITE: A more traditional Acropolis dust trail laid down by Sébastien Ogier in the Team Toyota Gazoo Racing-entered Yaris Rally 1 Hybrid.

Albert Park

Melbourne, Australia

Melbourne regards itself as the sporting capital of Australia, and the city owes that claim partly to its grand prix at Albert Park.

The race is part of a broad collection of major sporting and cultural events, including the Melbourne Cup, the Boxing Day Test match and the Australian Open tennis grand slam. But the grand prix is perhaps the biggest of all – it is a truly international occasion that ensures

Melbourne can compete for profile with Sydney, despite the aesthetic advantages bequeathed on the New South Wales city by the geography of its harbour, and the famous Opera House and Harbour Bridge.

The 'Australian Grand Prix' dates back to 1928 and became an F1 World Championship event for the first time in 1985, when Adelaide hosted the season finale. It was a popular venue, which

ran through a park and some of the streets of the city centre, and it staged a series of dramatic races, many of which were the climax to the season.

While Adelaide was enjoying a decade in the spotlight, a local businessman in Melbourne recognized what F1 could do for his city. Ron Walker, a proud Victorian who had been Lord Mayor of Melbourne and helped found the city's Crown Casino, did a deal with Bernie Ecclestone and stole the race from Adelaide. They moved it to the opening race of the season, and Melbourne has held the race in a vice-like grip ever since.

The first event in 1996 was controversial. A group of residents did not like the idea of their bucolic park – located in a delightful area between the city centre and the bohemian seaside town of St Kilda – being used for a motor race, and set up a protest group. It had little effect. The protests occasionally make some background noise, but on the whole, Melbourne embraces its grand prix.

OPPOSITE: Albert Park has the backdrop of Melbourne's Business District spires – seen here in 2022 with Nicholas Latifi's Williams.

LEFT: After the 2002 podium ceremony was over, Minardi owner Paul Stoddart and driver Mark Webber snuck up to celebrate their fifth place. They were the last points they would score all year, but they still beat Toyota.

As broadcaster and former racing driver Neil Crompton puts it: "It creates a vibrant city and it's good for business. They have done a really good job of doing big things. There is a crowd that goes to the Australian Grand Prix that we don't necessarily see at other motorsport events and it's really a Melbourne Cup on four wheels. It's a fashion event, a culinary event, a social event and it's also a great motorsport event. It's a tribute to the promoters and those that have kept it going."

The circuit runs around a lake, with the skyscrapers of downtown as a backdrop. The track is formed from the roads inside the park, which gives it a unique feel of part-street circuit, part-traditional race track. The original layout comprised 16 corners and was 5.30km (3.29 miles) long. It was tweaked for the event's return in 2022, after a two-year absence because of the pandemic, by cutting out

a couple of corners in the hope of promoting overtaking, and slightly shortened to 5.28km (3.28 miles). Overtaking still isn't easy, but nevertheless the track tends to produce good races. It is a real challenge with a good mix of corners, including the high-speed Esses of Turns 9 and 10, and walls up close always tempting drivers into accidents.

The list of Albert Park highlights is long. The infamous McLaren driver swap-around in 1998, when David Coulthard was asked to hand a victory to Mika Häkkinen who had misheard a message to come into the pits. A multi-car pile-up at the start in 2002, which helped Mark Webber finish fifth in a Minardi on his debut. As an Australian achieving such a strong result in an Australian-owned team, the organisers broke protocol and gave him his own moment on the podium after the main ceremony.

Five years later, Lewis Hamilton announced himself in 2007 by sweeping past McLaren teammate Fernando Alonso around the outside of the first corner. There was a one-two for one-year wonders Brawn on their debut in 2009. A huge somersaulting crash for Fernando Alonso in 2016. And a chaotic race strewn with three red flags in 2023.

The crowds are large – well over 100,000 attend the race. Melbourne is a universally popular destination for those in F1, despite the long flight. The grassy paddock behind the pits has a garden-party feel and the vibe is welcoming.

The race has lost its regular season-opening slot to the cash-rich Middle East – "cash is king" in F1, as Hamilton famously said at the 2020 event, which was cancelled before the cars had turned a wheel as the world headed at speed into Covid lockdown.

Ron Walker died in 2018, but his legacy lives on in the new contract Melbourne signed to host the Australian Grand Prix until 2035, and in which it is guaranteed to return to its former prestigious spot as the season opener at least four times.

The rest of the time, the season will start in Bahrain, or perhaps one day in Saudi Arabia. But no prizes for guessing where most people would rather kick off a new racing year if they had a choice that was not dictated by money. Melbourne is just about perfect.

OPPOSITE LEFT: The start of the penultimate Australian Grand Prix before Covid struck it from the calendar in 2020 and 2021.

OPPOSITE RIGHT: A solemn Andrew Westacott, CEO of the Australian Grand Prix Corporation, announces that the 2020 race is cancelled, while in the UK teams switch their focus to building ventilators.

ABOVE: In Melbourne, Turns 1 and 2 are the places for 'causing a collision' and the late-race restart of the 2023 grand prix didn't disappoint.

Autodromo Internazionale Enzo e Dino Ferrari

Imola, Italy

Imola will forever be associated with one weekend, and one man in particular – Ayrton Senna. The death of the Brazilian three-time world champion – arguably the greatest driver in history – on 1 May 1994 not only scarred the sport of Formula 1 forever, but sent reverberations around the world, leaving many millions reeling from the death of a racing driver who had transcended his sport and become an icon.

Senna died when he lost control of his Williams FW16 trying to stay ahead of a rival in a car he believed to be illegal. He had switched to Williams for 1994 expecting to return to the front after two years of watching first Nigel Mansell and then arch-rival Alain Prost sweep all before them in Williams's high-tech active suspension cars, the FW14B and FW15C.

But the ban on driver aids for 1994 caught Williams out, and Senna had endured a difficult first two races at the team, spinning out of his home race in Brazil and being taken out at the first corner in Aida, Japan. Having watched and listened to Michael Schumacher from that first corner, he also felt the German's Benetton was benefiting from a device that had been declared against the rules for that year – traction control.

Senna arrived at Imola already two wins down in the championship to a rival he had long before earmarked as someone who was good enough to cause him serious trouble, and determined to stop the rot.

But fate intervened during a weekend from hell. First, in Friday qualifying, Senna's compatriot

OPPOSITE: Patrick Tambay takes an emotional victory in the No.27 Ferrari the year after Gilles Villeneuve's death.'

BELOW LEFT: Ayrton Senna in the Williams pit during his final, fateful grand prix weekend in 1994.

BELOW: Villeneuve follows Pironi as they approach Variante Bassa chicane in the much-debated 1982 San Marino Grand Prix.

Rubens Barrichello suffered a violent accident at the fast chicane before the pits, taking off over a kerb and coming to rest upside down. Barrichello swallowed his tongue, but was rescued and was essentially uninjured, as Senna discovered earlier than most when he went to the medical centre to check on his colleague. When qualifying resumed, Senna took pole from Schumacher with a lap nearly 0.5 seconds faster than the German.

24 hours later, the weekend took an even darker turn when Roland Ratzenberger crashed in his Simtek after a front-wing failure at the high-speed Villeneuve kink and was killed instantly. Senna visited the scene of the accident, where F1's doctor and Senna's close confident Professor Sid Watkins, upon seeing how upset he was, asked the Brazilian why he didn't retire.

Race day unfolded as one of the worst in F1 history. There was a start-line crash, in which debris flew into the crowd and injured spectators. That led to a safety car. And a lap after the restart, Senna crashed catastrophically at the fast Tamburello left-hander, the corner before Villeneuve.

He had been straining to stay ahead of Schumacher, who unbeknownst to Senna was on a lighter fuel load and planning one more pit stop. Seeing the Benetton so close behind, Senna took a tighter line through what was normally a flat-out corner on the fateful lap.

The contention of the Williams team has always been that Senna hit bumps that he and teammate Damon Hill had been avoiding all weekend, which unsettled the car. They say this caused a stall in the underbody airflow, robbing Senna of downforce, and causing the loss of control.

Even then, Senna should have been all right. He was uninjured in the crash, save for a wound where the right-front suspension arm, torn off in the impact with the wall, had pierced his helmet and skull. Two months later, it was revealed that the Benetton did indeed have illegal software in it – hidden in a secret menu. The team escaped punishment because the FIA said it could not be proven it had been used.

Senna's death changed the image of Imola forever. Before that, it had been a bucolic place. The track's San Marino Grand Prix was held in spring. Usually the weather was balmy and warm. Filigree seed pods would float on the gentle breeze. The food was divine because it's in Emilia-Romagna, the heart of Italian cuisine. And the drive over the hills, past vineyards, to some of the secluded towns to the south, was postcard-perfect.

And then there was the track itself. The snaking, flat-out run from the Variante Bassa, past the pits, through Tamburello and Villeneuve, led to one of the best overtaking spots of the season, into the Tosa hairpin. The track climbed thereafter before plunging downhill through a fast left-hander known as Piratella, possibly the best corner on the track, through a wooded section to the fast right of Aqua Minerali, before rising again through an avenue of plane trees to Variante Alta. It then descended into a difficult downhill braking zone into the double left-hander of Rivazza, which sent the cars back to the pits.

But 1994 changed the circuit as well as the sport. Before Senna, there had been other, very nasty accidents at Tamburello. Nelson Piquet crashed his Williams there in 1987, and later said it took him months to fully recover. Gerhard Berger's Ferrari became engulfed in an inferno when he hit the wall during the 1989 race, and he suffered burns to his hands that forced him to miss the next race at Monaco. Michele Alboreto went off in testing in his Arrows in 1991.

Perhaps the fact that all these drivers had walked away from such heavy impacts had bred complacency. People said Tamburello could not be changed; the Santerno river ran up against the barrier, so the run-off could not be extended. But the safety drive instigated by FIA president Max Mosley after Senna's death changed all that.

OPPOSITE LEFT: Senna's teammate Damon Hill passes through Tamburello without incident during practice, where both drivers were avoiding a bump in the track.

OPPOSITE RIGHT: Rubens Barrichello, flanked by Eddie Jordan, returns to the paddock after his Friday accident.

ABOVE RIGHT: Roland Ratzenberger drives his Simtek over the kerbing, which is believed to have weakened the front wing.

RIGHT: Senna leads from Michael Schumacher as the cars approach the Tosa hairpin.

When F1 returned to Imola in 1995, chicanes had been inserted at both corners that had claimed lives the year before. It retained its joy as a driving challenge, but it had changed from one of the best tracks for racing to one of the worst. The new layout did, though, allow a defining race early in the career of Fernando Alonso, when in 2005 the Renault driver held off a charging Michael Schumacher's Ferrari with great skill despite his engine being down a cylinder for the entire final stint.

Old layout or new, there is something about Imola that generates drama. Its debut in F1 was as host of the Italian Grand Prix in 1980, when Monza was undergoing renovations. In that race, Gilles Villeneuve somehow escaped a huge accident unhurt at the corner that would later be named after him.

Two years later, Villeneuve was at the centre of one of Ferrari's greatest controversies when teammate Didier Pironi stole the victory from under the Canadian's nose despite Villeneuve

believing they had been given orders to hold position. Villeneuve's trust was broken and he vowed never to speak to Pironi again. He crashed to his death in qualifying at the very next race in Belgium two weeks later.

The following year, there was a moving twist to the tale. Villeneuve and Pironi were both gone – the Frenchman's career ended by horrific leg injuries suffered in a Hockenheim crash three months after Villeneuve's death. Villeneuve's replacement at Ferrari was Frenchman Patrick Tambay, one of his closest friends.

Tambay, his car bearing Villeneuve's famous number 27, qualified third, the same spot as Villeneuve had the year before. When he got to the grid he found a Canadian flag painted in front of his car. In the crowd, there were barriers demanding: 'Patrick, win it for Gilles.'

It didn't look as if it would be Tambay's day when Riccardo Patrese's Brabham passed the Frenchman for the lead late on. But then, as if

willed by the gods, Patrese crashed at Acque Minerali, and Tambay took the flag, to the raucous and emotional applause of the crowd, who were delighted that the Frenchman had beaten an Italian.

By 2006, the rising fees being demanded for F1 races had priced Imola out of the market and it fell off the calendar. It was thought unlikely ever to return, but the pandemic gave it another chance. When F1 was scouting for locations to fill up enough slots to make a serviceable season while the world was shut down for Covid-19, Imola was one of the venues to step forward, with help from the regional and national governments.

The race's new name, the Gran Premio dell'Emilia-Romagna Made In Italy, would win no prizes for brevity or style. But the track's return led to a terrific wet-dry race featuring wheel-to-wheel action between title contenders Lewis Hamilton and Max Verstappen and a high-speed crash between Mercedes driver Valtteri Bottas

and the Williams of George Russell, the man who went on to replace the Finn in his seat in 2022.

What had initially looked like a one-off race in an emergency turned out to be the start of something new. F1 president Stefano Domenicali grew up in Imola and once sold tickets at the race. He wanted the circuit to stay, and a new contract was signed until at least 2025. Whether it survives growing pressure to stop the expansion of a calendar that many in F1 believe has grown too long remains to be seen but, for now, Imola is back. Senna's statue at Tamburello remains a physical reminder of what was lost that terrible day in May 1994.

OPPOSITE LEFT: Charles Leclerc turns in to the Variante Alta with the distinctive stone pines of the Imola circuit beyond.

OPPOSITE RIGHT: Lewis Hamilton, using the pre-event media day to show off his latest fashion choice, re-acquaints himself with the Imola track at the exit of Rivazza.

ABOVE: A critical moment in the 2021 season, Lewis Hamilton and Max Verstappen head for the Tamburello chicane in the Emilia Romagna GP and Verstappen is in no mood to give way.

Autódromo José Carlos Pace

Interlagos, São Paulo, Brazil

Brazil's Autódromo José Carlos Pace race track – commonly known as the Interlagos circuit – throbs with the energy of the city that surrounds it.

São Paulo is an edgy place and this circuit is situated in one of its less salubrious districts. Turn off the Avenida das Nações Unidas from Morumbi onto the Avenida Interlagos and the road to the track crosses the Jurubatuba river, then climbs a hill past a favela.

One particular junction here is notorious for attacks on race personnel. And after a series of scares – Jenson Button and his crew narrowly escaped being held at gunpoint here in 2010 by jumping the lights and ramming their way through a traffic jam – an extra police presence has been put in place over grand prix weekends.

It's a city where you need to have your wits about you, but also one that positively buzzes with atmosphere – and the track reflects it.

Named after its location, which is nestled between two huge reservoirs (Interlagos translates as "between lakes") that supply the city with water, the track is a natural amphitheatre which fills with crowds who are passionate and partisan.

The modern 4.31km (2.67 mile) circuit is a truncated version of the original 7.96km (4.94 mile) layout that first held a world championship grand prix in 1973. Two of the old track's greatest corners, the long, banked, oval-style Turns 1 and 2 and the high-speed 180-degree Curva do Sol inside it, have been bypassed. The first is still there on the outside

of the new Turn 1-2-3, while the Curva Do Sol is now a car park. But the new track – much like at Spa in Belgium – retains the character of the old, curving up and down the hillside, and the second half of the lap is pretty much in its original form.

Old circuit or new, Interlagos is one of the few grand prix venues where it's possible to see almost the entire lap from many vantage points around the track. There are also expansive views of the sprawling metropolis beyond.

OPPOSITE: Lando Norris and Max Verstappen head towards Turn 1 at the start of the 2023 São Paulo Grand Prix.

BELOW LEFT: Emerson Fittipaldi became an even bigger national hero when he won the first two Brazilian grands prix at Interlagos; first with Lotus and here, in 1974, with McLaren.

ABOVE: Ayrton Senna only won his home grand prix twice – this was his final time in 1993.

The original race circuit, which was built in 1940, hosted only seven grands prix before the location of Brazil's race switched to Rio de Janeiro's Jacarepaguá track for nine years. But since returning to São Paulo in 1990, Interlagos has been a firm fixture on the calendar.

It has become famous as a stage for superlative racing action and has hosted many defining grands prix over the years, whether held early in the season, as was the case initially, or towards the end of the year, as it has been since 2004.

Interlagos will forever be linked with Ayrton Senna, who grew up in São Paulo, and after whom the circuit's first corner is named. The Senna 'S' is a steeply descending left-right which follows the long, curving pit straight and is one of the great overtaking spots on the grand prix calendar.

Fittingly, the track was the scene of one of Senna's most heroic victories, when he finally won his home grand prix after seven years of trying. In 1991, he was leading at Interlagos in the McLaren MP4-6 when his gearbox began to fail in the closing laps of the race, just as rain began to fall. Eventually, with a couple of laps remaining, he was left only with sixth gear. Riccardo Patrese – in the sole remaining Williams FW14, following Nigel Mansell's earlier retirement – was closing rapidly, but despite almost stalling in the slower corners, Senna held him at bay, to cross the line just under three seconds ahead. Exhausted, the Brazilian had to be lifted out of the car and driven in a medical car to the podium, where he struggled even to lift the trophy.

The list of great Interlagos moments is long. Rain in 2003 created a river across the track at Turn 3 which caught out many drivers, including the world champion Michael Schumacher. The race was red-flagged after 56 of the scheduled 71 laps following two massive accidents – Mark Webber

crashed his Jaguar coming onto the pit straight, and Fernando Alonso's Renault subsequently hit one of the Jaguar's errant wheels. The win was given to McLaren's Kimi Räikkönen on lap count back, only for the Jordan team to point out that officials had failed to take into account that their driver Giancarlo Fisichella was leading when the race was stopped. The Italian was awarded the win following an FIA appeal court hearing the following week.

Four years later, Lewis Hamilton's bid to become the only driver to win the title in his debut season foundered when his McLaren suffered a bizarre technical glitch. A hydraulic valve became temporarily blocked for 25 seconds before clearing, but not before he had dropped to 18th. In his subsequent climb back through the field, Hamilton fell two places short of the fifth place he needed to prevent Räikkönen, now at Ferrari, claiming the title thanks to his team inverting their two cars at their final pit stops and gifting him the win rather than teammate Felipe Massa.

A year later, Hamilton *did* win his first title, in even more remarkable circumstances. In a hectic climax during a late shower of rain, Hamilton went into the final lap one place short of the fifth place he needed to prevent Massa's imminent victory making him champion.

The Ferrari team celebrated as Massa crossed the line to win the race. But Hamilton on treaded rain tyres was closing on the Toyota of German Timo Glock, who had stayed out on slicks. The McLaren passed the Toyota as it slithered wide, grip-less out of the last corner to claim fifth place and the world championship.

In 2012, there was another dramatic title climax, this time between Red Bull's Sebastian Vettel and Ferrari's Fernando Alonso.

Vettel, heading into the race with a 13-point cushion, appeared comfortable. However, he made a bad start and collided with the Williams of Bruno Senna (Ayrton's nephew) at Turn 4

and dropped to 22nd, with his car's left-hand sidepod badly damaged.

Frantic photography of the injured car was analysed by the team and deemed survivable. Vettel moved up through the field, and managed to climb to sixth place, which was enough to give him the title despite Alonso finishing second to McLaren's Jenson Button.

Through 2019 and into 2020, the future of Interlagos as an F1 venue came under threat because of renewed interest from Rio, pushed by former president Jair Bolsonaro and given impetus by a dispute between the São Paulo promoter — a close ally of ousted F1 boss Bernie Ecclestone — and F1's new owners Liberty Media. But the Rio project was crushed by environmental opposition, even before Bolsonaro's downfall, and after F1 found a new promoter, Interlagos's future was secured with a new contract from 2021 that renamed it the São Paulo Grand Prix.

Interlagos has since lost its position as a regular title decider as other races have been placed later in the season. But the drama keeps coming; recent examples include Lewis Hamilton's incredible fightback to victory from an effective 25-place grid penalty in 2021, and Alonso's remarkable battle for third with Sergio Perez's Red Bull in 2023, in which the Aston Martin driver held off the faster Red Bull for 16 laps. Perez did finally manage to get in front, only for Alonso to re-pass the Mexican driver on the final lap of the race.

Few circuits could have served up races of such drama — title decider or not.

OPPOSITE: Lewis Hamilton heads uphill from Junção in 2008, in just about the same place that he overtook Timo Glock's Toyota to become World Champion.

TOP: It is exceptionally rare to have an incident-free race at Interlagos and one of the contributing factors is "the sudden downpour". Clouds gather during practice in 2023 as Alonso heads towards Descida do Lago .

ABOVE: Esteban Ocon, in the Racing Point and on quicker tyres, tries to unlap himself from Max Verstappen in 2018 through the Senna Esses. The incident led to a shoving match in the pits.

Autodromo Nazionale Monza

Monza, Italy

They call Monza 'La Pista Magica', and if that suggests a mix of eeriness and wonder, it's about right. To fully appreciate the unique mystery of this historic circuit, it's best to enter from the east, through the Porta San Giorgio early on a sunny September morning.

The entry road here feeds out through a second portico into a clearing beside the Golf Club Milano. Dappled, golden light filters through the Royal Park's famous 'whispering trees', witnesses to the 100 years of glory and tragedy that form the history of this most evocative of racing venues.

Continue through the trees, and a gap in a crash barrier leads you across a strip of asphalt. This is the back straight of Monza's banked oval, used for grands prix intermittently for the track's first 30-odd years. Next, descend through a small tunnel, this time under the modern grand prix circuit itself – specifically, the run from the Ascari chicane to the famous Parabolica, perhaps the greatest final corner on any circuit in motorsport.

In front now is a scene that is the very essence of the Italian Grand Prix weekend. There's a crossroads. Straight on is another tunnel, this one under the pit straight, leading to the other

entrances on the west side of the park. Left are the car parks for teams, drivers and media. Right is the entrance to the Formula 1 paddock, and beyond it souvenir and bookshops in which aficionados, especially those wearing rosso red, can lose themselves for hours.

Everything and everyone has to funnel through this crossroads. Every morning fans – the famous *tifosi* – gather here hoping for a glimpse of their heroes. When they get it, there is pandemonium in that very special, borderline anarchic Italian way. And when that hero is a Ferrari driver, well, the place erupts.

Ferrari and Monza are inextricably intertwined. The factory at Maranello is closer to Imola (see page 26), which itself has hosted many grands prix. But Monza is the *tifosi's* duomo and San Siro all rolled into one. These fans represent the continuation of a relationship, equal parts love affair and religious devotion, between the Italian nation and the Monza track that first resounded to the roar of engines in 1922.

Monza did not host the first Italian Grand Prix in 1921, that was at Montichiari, 60-odd miles (100km) to the west and just south of Brescia, the starting point for another Italian motor racing classic, the Mille Miglia (see page 146).

OPPOSITE: The *tifosi* flock to the podium after the 2023 race to celebrate Carlos Sainz's third place.

ABOVE: Winner of the 1924 Italian Grand Prix, Antonio Ascari with his son Alberto behind the wheel of his Alfa Romeo. Enzo Ferrari is visible between them, standing behind the car.

Monza was completed in time for the following year's race, and, with a handful of exceptions, it has been its home ever since. It has been through many forms: it started as a six-mile-long combination of the oval and modern grand prix track, then became a hybrid using bits of both for a while. The road course of today, without chicanes, was used for Formula 1's early years in the 1950s, before alternating intermittently with the combined track from 1955 until 1960, after which the road course became the standard.

Apart from the more recent addition of chicanes to slow the cars down, it remains pretty much unchanged to this day. And, despite the chicanes, its status as the fastest track of all remains.

Through that time, grand prix racing, Ferrari and Monza have become synonymous. That long history is so evocative partly because triumph and tragedy are interwoven there. Monza stands as a symbol of the entire sport and what it means.

It was just six years after the first Italian Grand Prix at Monza that disaster first struck. In 1928,

ABOVE: Six Ferraris line up before the 1956 Italian Grand Prix – five race cars and one 'training' car marked with a T.

ABOVE RIGHT: Peter Collins's Maserati on the Monza banking in 1955.

RIGHT: Niki Lauda in the Ferrari pit for the 1976 grand prix is handed notes by Mauro Forghieri. Competing in the race just forty days after his near-fatal crash at the Nürburgring was one of the single greatest acts of bravery F1 has ever seen.

Talbot's Emilio Materassi and Giulio Foresti's Bugatti tangled on the banking, Materassi's car swerved left, was launched into the air and smashed into the grandstand opposite the pits, killing the driver and 27 spectators. It was the worst accident in motor racing history until the 1955 Le Mans 24 Hours (see page 12).

Three years later, the race was remarkable for a different reason – it was more endurance event than grand prix, lasting 10 hours before the great Tazio Nuvolari secured victory. He shared an Alfa Romeo with Giuseppe Campari, an opera singer when he wasn't a racing driver, combining two great Italian passions in one man.

The Italian Grand Prix's centrality to Formula 1 may partly be because the sport itself was inherently Italian for a very long time. Apart from the age of the state-funded manufacturer teams of Mercedes and Auto Union from Nazi Germany in the 1930s, Italian teams were preeminent through the pre-war era of grand prix racing, and into the initial post-war period, too.

Racing resumed in 1947, and the first seven Italian Grands Prix were all won by Italian cars, three each for Alfa Romeo and Ferrari and one for Maserati. That time was both the end and the beginning of something special. Alfa Romeo, for so long a major force, faded away, and their place as the leading Italian team was taken by Ferrari, whose founder Enzo Ferrari had made his name racing and then running Alfa Romeos before setting up on his own.

The early 1950s marked the first dominant era for his team that, like its home race, has come in many ways to define Formula 1. Through 1952, Alberto Ascari's Ferrari 500 was unbeatable. He won six of seven races, missing the other because he was away racing at Indianapolis.

RIGHT: Gilles Villeneuve brings his Ferrari 126C into the pits during practice for the 1981 grand prix.

The following year, Ascari won five of seven races, but ironically it was at Monza where his and Ferrari's run came to an end. In a thrilling four-car slipstream battle, of the sort for which Monza was to become famous for the next 20 years, Ascari fought for much of the race with teammate Giuseppe Farina, and the Maseratis of Juan Manuel Fangio and Onofre Marimón.

It was Ascari's last race for Ferrari before he moved to the new Lancia team. Into the last lap, he led from Farina, Fangio and Marimón. They closed on some back-markers. Ascari knew he could not afford to back off or the race was lost, but he went into the last corner slightly too fast, and spun. Farina took to the grass in avoidance and a grateful Fangio swept by for his first win for two years.

Ascari was never to win another race. The Lancia move was a catastrophe. The team were underprepared and he barely raced at all in 1954 while Lancia struggled to ready their innovative side-tanked D50, which was not ready until the final race of the season.

The following year began promisingly, and Ascari was on course to win in Monaco, following the retirements of the dominant Mercedes of Fangio and Stirling Moss. But he made an error at the chicane on the 80th of 100 laps and the car plunged through the straw bales that marked the edge of the track and into the harbour, its driver having to swim to safety.

Four days later, Ascari was at Monza to watch his friend Eugenio Castellotti test a Ferrari sportscar. Ascari, who had broken his nose in his Monaco dip, was a superstitious man and considered his

ABOVE LEFT: The Williams reserve driver Jean-Louis Schlesser canons into Senna's McLaren at the first chicane in 1988.

LEFT: A classic Darren Heath photograph of Monza's main straight taken from Parabolica, now renamed for Michele Alboreto.

light blue helmet a lucky charm. Not intending to drive that day, he had left it at home. Then he expressed a wish to try the 750 Monza, and donned Castellotti's helmet.

On his third lap, he crashed, inexplicably and catastrophically. The car skidded, turned on its nose and somersaulted twice, at the high-speed left-hander known as Vialone. Ascari was gone. The corner where he lost his life was later named for him.

Five years later, Monza marked the end of another era. Fangio won the drivers' title for Ferrari in 1956, driving one of the D50s the team had taken over when Lancia fell on hard times. But the late 1950s were a bleak period for Italy's now-preeminent team. And by 1960 Ferrari had been left behind. The British teams, led by Cooper, had shown the future — it was mid-engined.

Ferrari had obstinately stuck to his preferred front-engined philosophy for too long, but the car did have one strength, its engine. And that provided an opportunity. For the previous three years, the Italian Grand Prix had been run on the road course. But for 1960, the organisers decided to revive the combined road and oval track, to the annoyance of the British teams. With a much greater opportunity to stretch the car's legs, Phil Hill took Ferrari's sole victory of the year. It was the final win for a front-engined car in Formula 1 history.

By 1961, Ferrari had joined the rear-engined revolution, and the gorgeous 156 'shark-nose' dominated the season. Their driver Wolfgang von Trips came to Monza leading the points, with Hill second. One or the other was going to be champion.

Von Trips took pole, leading a Ferrari one-two-three-four. But on the second lap of the race, disaster struck. Von Trips, who had been slow

off the line, collided with Jim Clark's Lotus and careened into a spectator bank. Along with the driver, 15 spectators were killed. The race was not stopped, and Phil Hill won it, clinching the title in the process.

Through the 1960s, Monza consolidated its reputation as a place for slipstreaming battles, and in those days before aerodynamic downforce, many of its high-speed corners were among the sport's most extreme challenges.

In 1967, Clark, now a two-time champion, demonstrated his and the Lotus 49's superiority in awe-inspiring style, when he fell a lap behind after a problem in the early stages, and proceeded to make up the lap and re-take the lead, only to run out of fuel in the final tour.

TOP: Monza has one of the longest runs to the first corner, the Variante del Rettifilio, and it carries a strong risk of contact.

ABOVE: Max Verstappen barged into the Mercedes of Lewis Hamilton at the first corner in 2021, with the rear wheel of the Red Bull striking Hamilton's helmet.

With the dawn of the 1970s, tragedy and triumph were combined in one terrible event. In 1970, Jochen Rindt was killed in practice after a brake shaft sheared on his Lotus 72 as he approached Parabolica. The Austrian, who had dominated the second half of the season, was later confirmed as the sport's only posthumous world champion.

The following year, Peter Gethin led five cars across the line to seal the closest finish in F1 history, his BRM finishing just 0.01 seconds ahead of Ronnie Peterson's March, and 0.61 seconds covering the first five cars. But as the slipstreaming era reached its zenith, it also reached its end. This was the height of Jackie Stewart's campaign to get the sport to take safety seriously. And the following year, chicanes were inserted before Curva Grande, the Lesmos and at Ascari.

By the mid-1970s, the *tifosi* had been waiting a decade to see a Ferrari win at Monza, the last time being John Surtees's victory on his way to the drivers' championship in 1964. But under the leadership of Luca Cordero di Montezemolo and with Niki Lauda as lead driver, the team were revived and dominated the 1975 season. Clay Regazzoni duly delivered the long-awaited home win as Lauda came home third in a wet race to clinch Ferrari's first drivers' title for 11 years.

But it was the following year when Lauda etched himself into motorsport folklore. Apparently running away with a second consecutive title, the Austrian crashed inexplicably at the Nürburgring. Trapped in the burning wreckage, Lauda had to be saved by fellow drivers. In hospital with third-degree burns and damaged lungs, he was given the last rites. Forty days later, in one of the greatest acts of bravery any sport has ever seen, he returned to the cockpit of his Ferrari and finished fourth at Monza. After the race, he gingerly peeled his balaclava from blood-soaked bandages covering still-raw wounds on his face.

Two years later, with Lauda's exit from Ferrari – having won a second title and fallen out with the owner – the *tifosi* had a new hero.

BELOW LEFT: An aerial view of Monza's royal park from 2021 shows that the banked oval is still intact. The road course crosses underneath as it heads for the Ascari Chicane before turning left onto the back straight. Many of these trees were lost in the summer gales of 2023.

BELOW: The Monza qualifying trio from 2023: Max Verstappen joins pole-sitter Carlos Sainz and Charles Leclerc as Ferrari celebrate 75 years in business with dedicated overalls, along with an anniversary livery for the car.

OPPOSITE: Carlos Sainz's Ferrari on the grid on pole position before the 2023 race. The flypast by the Frecce Tricolori happening in defiance of an ordinance from F1 that such things should not happen as the sport tries to establish its green credentials.

Gilles Villeneuve had joined the team as Lauda's replacement and his cavalier style soon won him a legion of fans.

In 1978, Villeneuve fought for the on-track lead throughout the race with Mario Andretti's much-faster Lotus, although both were penalised for a jumped-start, handing the win, ironically, to Lauda. Andretti sealed the title that day, though it was a triumph he could not celebrate, as his teammate Ronnie Peterson died in the night after a first-corner pile-up at the start of the race.

A year later, in 1979, Villeneuve further secured his support in Italy when he dutifully followed team orders and stuck to the word he had given his teammate, to sit behind Jody Scheckter as the South African won the race to secure his own Ferrari world title.

Villeneuve expected his time would come, but four years later he, too, was gone. His death at Belgium's Circuit Zolder in May 1982 led to another iconic Ferrari-Monza moment. With Villeneuve's replacement Patrick Tambay struggling with back injuries and a constructors' title to be won, Ferrari called up Andretti for the final two races of the year in Italy and Las Vegas.

Andretti, an American racing legend, but born in Motovun, Croatia (then known as Montona, and part of Istria in the Kingdom of Italy), disembarked from his flight from the US at Malpensa airport, arms aloft for the TV cameras, with a Ferrari cap on his head, and then promptly stuck the car on pole for the race. The grand prix was won by Renault's René Arnoux, ahead of Tambay and Andretti. But that was fine with the *tifosi* – the Frenchman would be joining Ferrari for 1983.

Like the 1960s, the 1980s were a bleak period for Ferrari but in 1988 they received an unexpectedly poignant present. McLaren-Honda had swept all before them that year, winning

every race. Enzo Ferrari died on 14 August and then, at the first Italian GP following his death, it seemed fate intervened. McLaren failed to win for the only time that year. Alain Prost suffered engine problems and then Ayrton Senna crashed out after tangling with a back marker in the race's closing stages, handing Gerhard Berger and Michele Alboreto a one-two for Ferrari.

In the 30-odd years since then, it has been more famine than feast for the *tifosi*. There were six home wins in 11 years through the Michael Schumacher era of 1996–2006. But since then, only Fernando Alonso in 2010 and Charles Leclerc in 2019 have won for Ferrari at Monza.

Each win, though, was a classic in its own right. In 2010, Alonso won a flat-out battle with Jenson Button's McLaren, while Leclerc had to

get his elbows out to hold off Lewis Hamilton's dominant Mercedes in 2019.

Both celebrated on the new podium, the drivers on a pedestal – both literal and figurative – that juts out over the *tifosi* following their post-race track invasion. Any driver who experiences the outpouring of joy that greets their victory in red at the sport's most evocative venue will tell you it is a career highlight that's hard to surpass.

And the fans? Well, they might just take the opportunity to liberate a souvenir or two from any car unfortunate enough to have been abandoned trackside during the race.

Monza – madly chaotic, wonderfully evocative, unfailingly moving. There is nothing else quite like it.

Bahrain International Circuit

Sakhir, Bahrain

The Middle East has become central to so much in sport. Whether it be convulsing golf with a rival tour, holding major boxing matches, or signing footballing megastars to play in domestic leagues, oil money is reshaping the sporting landscape in pursuit of the desire to manipulate the global image of a few small, but very rich and influential, countries.

So it seems strange to think that it is not so very long ago that the region was almost invisible in sporting terms. The event that began to change all that was the Bahrain Grand Prix.

The innovator was the country's Crown Prince, Sheikh Salman bin Hamad Al Khalifa, who saw the potential in his country hosting Formula 1 and was the force behind the Bahrain International Circuit – the grand prix is his pet project.

Before the tiny island off the eastern coast of Saudi Arabia held a grand prix, it was known chiefly for being the base of the US Navy's Fifth Fleet. Prince Salman saw an opportunity to put his country on the map, and make it a place with which the West would want to do

business, whether it be banking, holidays, or perhaps motorsport.

The track first held a race in 2004 and has since become a staple of the F1 calendar. By the 2020s, in a change precipitated by the pandemic, it had become the default first race of the season. It's a position it will hold for the foreseeable future, other than a handful of years when the timing of the Muslim holy month of Ramadan will allow Australia to step into its former spot.

Famously surfaced with aggregate shipped in from Shropshire in the UK, and costing a reputed $150m, Sakhir is an essentially uninspiring circuit – point-and-squirt, long straights, few demanding corners – whether in the standard 5.41km (3.36 mile) format used for the grand prix, the longer 6.29km (3.9 mile) 'endurance' layout which hosted it in 2010 at the Crown Prince's behest, or the shorter outer layout which held one of two consecutive races at the end of the Covid-hit 2020 season.

Visually, too, it is unappealing, situated half an hour south of the capital Manama in scrubby, rocky desert near an oil field and an airbase.

OPPOSITE: Sergio Perez in practice for the 2023 grand prix amid the barren rock surrounds of the Sakhir circuit.

LEFT: When Formula 1 held its breath... Romain Grosjean crashes into the barriers, which separated owing to the extreme force. It split the car in two, puncturing the fuel tank and creating an inferno from which the driver emerged with only minor injuries.

Everywhere around is beige, bleached by the sun or blasted by sand. Turning it into a twilight race, a decision made for 2014, transformed it. With fairy lights draped around the palm trees in the paddock, and the environs invisible, the track's aesthetic appeal is exponentially improved.

The decision has been repaid with some edge-of-the-seat races, most notably in 2014, when Mercedes drivers Lewis Hamilton and Nico Rosberg staged a gloves-off battle for the win, and the buzz created by Fernando Alonso's return to the front with Aston Martin – and superlative passes on Hamilton and Ferrari's Carlos Sainz – in 2023. The track will forever be famous as the place where Romain Grosjean escaped like a phoenix from the flames of a horrifying fiery accident in 2020.

While a lack of thrills has been transformed with a change of race time, there are more serious issues for the Bahrain circuit that won't go away as easily: it is forever in the shadow of the claims of human rights abuses. The popular uprising of the Arab Spring forced the race to be cancelled in 2011 and there was controversy after F1 returned a year later, when some team personnel were caught in a riot on the motorway.

Central Bank of Bahrain

HALF DINAR

The issue of human rights comes up every year F1 goes back, and Bahrain has since been followed by three further races in the Middle East – Abu Dhabi, Qatar and Saudi Arabia. Two are held at twilight, two at night. A cynic might say that, inside the F1 paddock, the trees and the lights and the sense of hospitality and warmth for the privileged, not to mention the night skies, close off the outside world and make it easier to put the attendant controversy to the back of the sport's collective mind.

But whatever one might think about it, the Middle East as a sporting powerhouse is here to stay. And it was Crown Prince Salman who opened that door.

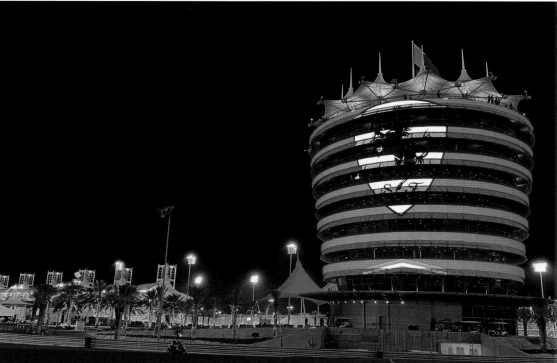

OPPOSITE: An aerial view of the Bahrain circuit from 2004 when it became the first Middle Eastern circuit to host a Formula 1 grand prix.

TOP LEFT: The tricky downhill Turns of 9 and 10, a favourite place for front tyre locking in the race.

TOP RIGHT: The importance of the 20-year race can be gauged by the circuit's inclusion on Bahraini currency.

BOTTOM: Undoubtedly, the transformation to an evening race has boosted the popularity of the grand prix. The shift of pre-season testing to Bahrain has eliminated the vagaries of weather sometimes faced at Circuit de Catalunya.

Baku City Circuit

Baku, Azerbaijan

Azerbaijan set a new record for a fee for a race when it agreed to pay $75m a year to join the Formula 1 calendar from 2016. It was the latest example of a regime with an unsavoury reputation centred on human rights abuses using sport to launder its global image. No surprise, then, that the Azerbaijan Grand Prix presents the best face of the country's capital, Baku.

The 6.3km (3.7 mile) street circuit incorporates two parts of the centre of the city. Most of it negotiates a series of straights and right-angled corners through a new town modelled on the grand boulevards of European cities such as Paris and Barcelona. The western end of the circuit, meanwhile, circumnavigates Baku's medieval castle. Further west, the gleaming skyscrapers of the central business district; to the south the glistening Caspian Sea, along the shore of which the long pit 'straight' runs.

In the first sector, the corners, predominantly left-handers, some right, are all more or less the same. A fiddly, ever-so-tight chicane then launches the cars uphill towards the castle section, which leads to possibly the best corner – the tricky, downhill Turn 15, approached at high speed through three kinks, where it is all too easy to misjudge the entry and collect the wall on the exit.

The close walls, high speeds and big braking points seem to bring the best out of Charles Leclerc, as close to a Baku specialist as it gets. He took pole positions for Ferrari in 2021, 2022

and 2023, despite only having the fastest car in the middle one of those years.

But while Baku is no Spa or Suzuka, it does tend to produce drama. The combination of tight corners and long straights means a low-downforce set-up and slipstreaming, and accidents are common. With accidents on street circuits come safety cars, and with safety cars comes pandemonium.

The first event was surprisingly dull, the F1 drivers all scared into conservatism by a harum-

scarum Formula 2 race on the support bill. But since then the race has been characterized by chaos. In 2017, Sebastian Vettel deliberately banged wheels with Lewis Hamilton, the German erroneously thinking his title rival had given him a 'brake test' while they lapped behind a safety car. In 2018, the Red Bull drivers Max Verstappen

OPPOSITE: Kevin Magnussen's Haas in free practice before the 2023 Azerbaijan Grand Prix.

ABOVE: With his brake balance on the wrong setting, Lewis Hamilton locks up and goes straight on at the restarted 2021 grand prix, handing the race to Sergio Perez.

LEFT: Expecting the unexpected in 2023, would mean a Sergio Perez victory and though the Mexican did indeed win the GP, Verstappen used the race to fully understand his set-up options on the RB19. Absheron is the name of the peninsula on which Baku is located.

BELOW: Two images from 2023 incorporating views of the Baku Fortress. The track narrows to less than 8 metres (26 ft) in this section.

OPPOSITE: An image from 2018 as the two Red Bulls brake heavily for Turn 1. Daniel Ricciardo (3) avoided hitting Max Verstappen (33) this time round, but when they collided later in the race Christian Horner asked his drivers to apologise to the team.

and Daniel Riccardo crashed out of the race together when Verstappen moved late in the braking zone.

And in 2021 Verstappen lost a commanding victory for Red Bull to a tyre failure, before Hamilton threw away a victory he would have inherited – and a chance to make up ground in their title fight – when he left his brakes on the wrong setting at the restart and speared into the escape road.

There was a time, after Liberty Media took over F1, that the race looked under threat. The new US owners questioning the value of a race in the country against the backdrop of increasing competition for races and pressure to keep calendar expansion under control.

But money talks in Formula 1, and in 2023 Azerbaijan signed a new deal to keep the race until at least 2026.

Bathurst 1000

New South Wales, Australia

Jim Richards had just won the 1992 Bathurst 1000, his fifth victory in a race that had built its reputation on madness and drama and had just delivered perhaps its craziest ever finish. But as he stood on the podium, the crowd were booing him and shouting obscenities.

A few moments earlier, Richards had been told that his friend Denny Hulme, the 1967 Formula 1 world champion, had died of a heart attack at the wheel of his BMW M3 during the race. Amid all the conflicting emotions coursing through him, Richards's reaction to the baying crowd was to tell them what he thought of them. His speech has gone down in motorsport history.

"This is bloody disgraceful," the New Zealander said. "I'll keep racing but, I tell you what, this is going to remain with me for a long time. You're a pack of arseholes."

This was — in the words of former racing driver and now leading broadcaster Neil Crompton, who was on the podium that day after finishing third — the "peak aggro moment" in the history of a race that has come to define Australian motorsport.

Bathurst is famous for all the right reasons — and all the wrong ones too. The circuit is magnificent. For Richards, who has won the race seven times — behind only the legendary nine-time winner Peter Brock in the all-time list — it is "definitely one of the best tracks in the world". And it has a tendency to produce exciting, topsy-turvy races, where pretty much anything can happen — and does.

ABOVE: Mark Skaife (left) and Jim Richards (right) after winning 'The Great Race' in 2002.

OPPOSITE: The grid lines up for the start of the Supercars Bathurst 1000 at Mount Panorama Circuit in October 2023.

Australian broadcasters made the race famous across the globe through innovative television coverage in the 1980s, which saw the pioneering of in-car cameras and microphones on the drivers. As long ago as 1981, there was a big crash at the top of the hill, and the drivers stopped on track were talking about the accident on television before they had even got out of their cars. It was a revelation — and a revolution.

But the antics of some of the spectators, who developed obsessive, tribal support for the rival Holden and Ford car brands, were for a long

time, in Crompton's words, "everything rotten that you would have read about at the bad, old rock concerts".

The Mount Panorama circuit is 6.16km (3.83 miles) long and climbs and descends the eponymous hill on public roads that were first built in 1938 by the chief engineer of the city of Bathurst, and immediately started holding races. "Either by good luck, good measure or serendipity," Crompton says, "he has drawn this epic race track."

The most famous section is up on 'the Mountain', where there is a sequence of daunting, fast corners, with next to no run-off. Most famous of all, perhaps, is Skyline, where the track reaches its highest point by turning right over a crest at high speed, fast and blind with walls on either side, then immediately left as it starts a steep plunge into the Esses, and then the Dipper, the track swerving left and right, left and right as it cascades down from the summit.

For a long time, the track boundaries at Skyline were rock faces; it's been made safer since, but it's still a track where crazy things happen – both during the racing and in the spectator enclosures.

In 1980, the race of Dick Johnson – another celebrated driver who has won the event three times – was ended when he hit a rock that had rolled down on to the track. Urban legend says it was pushed there by two inebriated fans. In 2004, Richards's race was ended when he hit a kangaroo that had strayed on to the track.

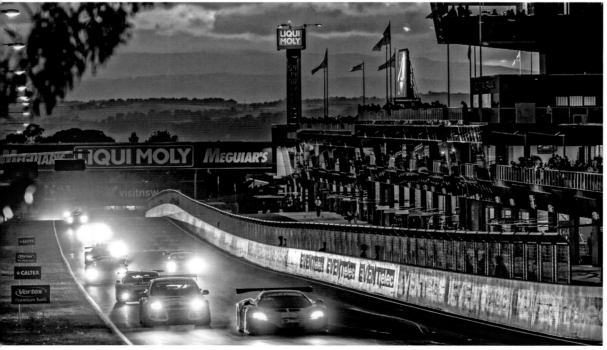

ABOVE LEFT: Kiwi touring car ace Shane van Gisbergen (SVG) takes Murray's Corner at Bathurst in his Red Bull/Ampol Racing Chevrolet Camaro.

LEFT: Though known for its V8 Supercars race, there are also 12-hour and 24-hour races at the Mount Panorama Circuit.

OPPOSITE: The tight, challenging downhill curves of Bathurst's famous Dipper.

Bathurst has made heroes whose names are known to motorsport fans worldwide – along with Brock, Richards and Johnson, Craig Lowndes has won it seven times, Larry Perkins and Mark Skaife six, Richards's son Steve five.

There have been multiple pile-ups, thrilling race finishes, drama, intrigue, politics and – in that infamous event in 1992 – a race stopped because of a torrential downpour. It ended with a car being declared the winner despite the fact that Richards had crashed it into two other cars on the Conrod Straight on the way back down the mountain, having lost control on slick tyres in the wet.

That decision, based on a common rule in motorsport where a red-flagged race has its result declared from the end of the last completed lap before it was stopped – was part of the reason for the abuse Richards received on the podium that year.

But some of it was also because Richards and co-driver Skaife were driving a Nissan Skyline R32 GT-R, a car known as 'Godzilla', which had utterly dominated the Australian touring car championship, effectively eliminating competition and rendering Ford and Holden bit-part players.

The crowd were already booing when the third-place drivers climbed on to the podium, whereupon Crompton – Richards's teammate in another Nissan – mouthed to the crowd that they could get lost (in more direct language) and gave them the finger.

Second-placed Johnson wound them up further with some choice remarks about a crashed car winning the race. On the top step, meanwhile, Skaife had unopened beer cans in each jacket pocket and was steeling to throw them back at the crowd, before eventually thinking better of it.

Richards recalls: "I was surprised it was so venomous, you might say, where everybody started chanting. I thought we'd get a few boos and a few guys calling out, but it was massive, and the beer cans being thrown at you; empty ones, full ones, it didn't really matter.

"It wasn't planned that I would say anything but I just felt spur of the moment that I needed to tell them what they were up to."

This being Australia, though, everyone ended up having a sense of humour about it. The following year, two guys turned up with T-shirts bearing the slogan: 'I'm an arsehole, Jim told me.' They got Richards to sign them. All of this might sound more akin to football fans than motor-racing fans, but the Bathurst crowd back then was unlike any other. The spectator areas up on the mountain were notorious for drunkenness and debauchery. Australian former Formula 1 driver Mark Webber says: "There was a period where it got a little bit out of hand. It was not a place for a female."

Steve Richards says that at its worst it was "anarchy" up on the mountain. "It evolved to the point were people were taking old cars up and going loose in the back of the campgrounds and doing burn-outs, and setting fire to them," Richards says. "The legend was that guys were driving up in their rental cars from Sydney and going up to have a look at the top of the mountain to see what all the fuss was about, but then getting pulled over or directed into these burn-out areas and being forced to be part of the show. But then having their car flipped over with them in it, pulling them out of the car and then setting fire to these random cars.

"We all know that people were badly hurt up there from cars in the middle of the night getting too close to tents. Legend has it that a couple of people actually perished up there from stupidity, blowing up plastic toilets with dynamite."

The rivalry between fans of Ford and Holden was part of this mix. The parent companies may have been based in America – this was Ford v General Motors, the oldest industrial rivalry in the US – but they built the cars for the local market in Australia. Fans developed an attachment to one brand or the other. You were either a "Ford bloke" or a "Holden bloke" – and never the twain would meet. "People would argue and fight," Crompton says. "It's pretty radical when you think about it now."

This was intensified as the brands started to build souped-up, homologation special road cars, to enhance their chances of victory at Bathurst. And in the end, the authorities stepped in to bring an end to the excess, both in the car market and at the race track.

In road-car sales, Steve Richards says: "All of a sudden the legislators said, 'No way, this is crazy.

People on the roads are going to kill themselves. People were going up the Hulme highway from Melbourne to Sydney at 200km/h (124mph) and writing themselves off the road."

In 2009, restrictions on the amount of alcohol that fans could take up the mountain were introduced – with a limit of 24 cans per day. The response of some fans? To go up there weeks in advance with coolers full of beer, and bury them so they could dig them up when it came to race week.

Since then, though, the gentrification of what back in the 1970s was a working class, agricultural area, the creeping professionalism of motor racing, and a firm hand from the authorities has changed the character of the spectator enclosures.

"It has been better for the event," Crompton says. "That has gone and now you get a lot of families up there experiencing it with young kids.

"There is still an element of freedom for people to sort of do things that at most other racetracks you probably wouldn't be able to do, but they have stopped all the looseness. By all accounts it's still a hell of a lot of fun for people who go and experience the race up there, but you can't set fire to anything up there any more after the race."

The track has been made safer, too, with some of the rock walls moved back, but it remains a magnificent challenge. The darker edges of the event have been smoothed over, but as Webber puts it: "Bathurst is the race that captivated the nation, and still does."

OPPOSITE: An aerial view of Mount Panorama, with cars ascending from the right.

ABOVE LEFT: The climb up to Mount Panorama through Reid Park, Sulman Park and McPhilamy Park.

TOP: Jason Plato (left) partnered the most successful Bathurst exponent Peter Brock for his last Great Race in 2004.

RIGHT: There is little need for Surf Life Saving on Mount Panorama, but some fans still come equipped.

Brands Hatch

Kent, England

Brands Hatch, just off the M20 motorway near Sevenoaks in Kent, is one of the greatest race tracks in the United Kingdom. It has faded somewhat since its glory days as co-host of the British Grand Prix, holding the race in even-numbered years between 1964 and 1986, alternating with Silverstone. But it was then and remains now a drivers' favourite.

It was very different in character from Silverstone. In contrast with the flat landscape of the Northamptonshire plateau and the straights and fast corners of the former airfield there, Brands Hatch is noted for its topography.

The shorter 'Indy' circuit swoops around a natural amphitheatre, and starts with one of motorsport's greatest corners, Paddock Hill Bend, a fiendishly challenging fast right-hander that drops away on entry and then falls seemingly almost vertically into a hollow through its exit.

Perhaps the most famous race was a hot-tempered affair in the searing summer of 1976, when a raucous crowd protested loudly at the idea James Hunt's McLaren might be prevented from taking the restart of a race that had been red-flagged after a collision between him and the rival Ferraris at Paddock on the first lap. Hunt drove his McLaren back to the pits for repairs via an access road and not the circuit.

Chants in favour of Hunt started, together with a hail of beer cans, and the stewards decided to let Hunt take the restart. He repaid the crowd's support by passing Lauda, his title rival, to take victory, only for Ferrari to protest and for officials to award the race to Lauda several weeks down the line.

It was the start of a heady second half of the 1976 season, in which Lauda suffered his famous fiery accident, came back bravely after missing just two races, and Hunt won the title by a point after Lauda withdrew from the soaking finale at Fuji in Japan.

There was a time when the UK had two F1 races a year. For a few years, Brands Hatch held the Race of Champions in the spring. Then in 1983 and 1985, it hosted a second grand prix, the European. Nigel Mansell took his maiden F1 victory in the 1985 race, narrowly beating teammate Keke Rosberg. A year later, at the British GP, held at Brands Hatch on a glorious summer's day, he passed his Williams teammate Nelson Piquet to win and cement his status as a national hero.

Nowadays, Brands Hatch, despite restrictions on the number of events that can be held because of nearby housing, thrives as a host of national racing and lower-tier international events as part of former F1 driver Jonathan Palmer's Motor Sport Vision conglomerate.

OPPOSITE: Nigel Mansell (5) starts from the front row alongside Ayrton Senna in the JPS Lotus for the final Formula 1 race in 1986.

BELOW LEFT: A drone shot looking down on the pit straight at Brands Hatch with Paddock Hill Bend far left.

BELOW: James Hunt at Brands Hatch during the tumultuous grand prix of 1976.

Buddh International Circuit

Greater Noida, Uttar Pradesh, India

Bernie Ecclestone, who ran Formula 1 for 40 years until handing over the keys to Liberty Media in 2017, had an ambition to hold a grand prix in India from about 1995. It was a vision realised – briefly – with the Buddh International circuit, which hosted races for three years from 2011–13. The race came to Ecclestone somewhat out of the blue. He had recruited Vicky Chandhok – son of the man behind India's first international race circuit in Madras (see page 140) and father of racing driver Karun – as his eyes and ears in India, and had asked him to give a once-over to every potential project as they popped up.

A number did, but none made the grade. Until one day Chandhok's phone rang. In the mid-2000s, he and the billionaire businessman Vijay Mallya – soon to buy an F1 team and name it Force India – were trying to get a street race in New Delhi off the ground. The plan was for it to focus on India Gate, and the locations of the annual Republic Day Parade. Then Ecclestone phoned up and said some guys had put $20m into an escrow account and signed a contract for a grand prix. The people behind the project weren't just anyone; it was the Jaypee Group, one of India's biggest conglomerates, with interests across the economy ranging from engineering and construction to hospitality and sport. This was to be their first foray into international motorsport.

Ecclestone had sent them an initial contract, expecting it to be the start of a negotiation, and, to his surprise, they had just signed it. The deal assigned almost everything from which it was possible to make money – naming rights for every corner to the track and all hospitality

income – to Ecclestone. He even had the rights to 5,000 tickets – usually the main way for tracks to earn money in the Ecclestone era. The seeds of the financial problems that would eventually bring the race down had already been sown.

The idea of the Gaur family, who run Jaypee, was to create a purpose-built track on agricultural land in Greater Noida, to the south-east of Delhi. It was to be part of a new sport city, with residential and business properties just off the recently completed Delhi to Agra motorway, which Jaypee was also to build as part of the package of rights it had negotiated with the government. The idea was that the property sales would eventually pay for everything. And the model for that was a new city called Gurgaon, near the international airport on the other side of Delhi, where at the time property prices were exploding, increasing thirty-fold in a few years.

The site for what was to become the 5.13km (3.18 mile) Buddh circuit was initially just a bunch of rice-padi fields. Four-wheel drive vehicles were required to reach it. Ecclestone obliged the organisers to use his favoured architect Hermann Tilke, and a huge construction village was set up. Accommodation was provided. Money was no object. They wanted to do the job right.

OPPOSITE: Jean-Éric Vergne learns the circuit during his first appearance at the Buddh circuit for Toro Rosso in 2012.

TOP RIGHT: Jenson Button, then driving for McLaren-Mercedes, in the almost-obligatory auto-rickshaw photo opportunity.

RIGHT: Sebastian Vettel wins the debut Formula 1 Indian Grand Prix in 2011.

As is often the case, the build went right to the line. With a week to go before the first race in 2011, the asphalt on the main straight had still not been laid, because the cranes lifting the grandstand roof were still in use. It eventually went down on the Tuesday, three days before F1 cars first took to the track.

Shortly before the race, Ecclestone's lieutenant Pasquale Lattuneddu went out to India to check on progress. He noticed there were no hospitality boxes. He and Chandhok phoned Bernie.

"Where are the commentary boxes?" Ecclestone asked? On top of the grandstand, he was told. There were 52. "Right," Ecclestone said, "Those are now the hospitality boxes". "What will we do with the commentators," he was asked? "I don't know," Ecclestone said. "Put them in an underground bunker, I don't give a shit." And he hung up.

When they turned up for the race, the TV companies found their commentary boxes buried in the main pit building – no windows, next to the kitchen. The race, though, went ahead without hiccup, as it did for the succeeding two years. This was the height of Red Bull's first period of domination, and Sebastian Vettel won all three editions. In 2012, it was the last of four consecutive victories by the German following a key upgrade on the

car which allowed him to overhaul what had at one stage been a large points lead built up by Fernando Alonso driving one of the greatest seasons in history in an uncompetitive Ferrari.

On television, the races looked much like any other on one of Tilke's tracks, even if the Uttar Pradesh smog gave the pictures a unique, hazy feel. Behind the scenes, though, trouble was brewing, and the race was increasingly in jeopardy.

There were two main problems – both of them financial. The first was tax. The Indian government saw F1 as an entertainment, and therefore not due the normal tax exemption for sporting events. There was entertainment tax, legal licence tax, food tax, and then tax on F1 – on drivers, on teams, and on and on. The money was deducted at source, off the rights fee. In theory, F1 should have been able to claim it back – even now, it is owed about $20m from the Indian tax authorities, which it never expects to see again.

On top of that, the organisers were beginning to see the race as a black hole for money. Jaypee spent $400m building the track. Rights fees and running costs were in the region of $50–60m a year. The numbers simply did not add up.

Before the 2013 race, Chandhok flew to London with a message from the organisers for Ecclestone. The race fee that year should have been around $42m – the original fee in 2011 had been $35m, with a 10% annual escalator. Chandhok had been told to tell Ecclestone they would pay $25m – take it or leave it. Ecclestone took it – and then cancelled the rest of the contract.

With the race gone, real estate values crashed, and Jaypee had to sell off a hydro-electric power plant to recover some of the debt. Buddh still exists, though, and in September 2023 it successfully hosted MotoGP, its first world championship event since the demise of F1. It would take the political and financial stars to align, but who knows? Maybe one day Formula 1 could even go back to India.

OPPOSITE TOP: Shades of Shanghai and Sepang? The final corner/pit lane entrance at Buddh has a strong resemblance to other Tilke-designed circuits. Here, Kimi Räikkönen heads off to the pits in his 2012 Lotus-Renault.

OPPOSITE BOTTOM: Fernando Alonso (Ferrari) follows Michael Schumacher in the less-than-beautiful Mercedes WO3.

BELOW LEFT: Pole-sitter Sebastian Vettel leads teammate Mark Webber at the 2012 race. Vettel completed the second of his trio of Indian wins.

BELOW: Very much a precursor to the modern idea of coupling a concert to a grand prix, Metallica were lined up to play in 2011 as part of the grand prix weekend celebrations but the gig was cancelled at the last minute.

Circuit of the Americas

Austin, Texas, USA

It would be wrong to say that Taylor Swift made the United States Grand Prix in Austin, Texas, but the global pop phenomenon certainly helped prove the concept that transformed the event from slightly wobbly beginnings to becoming Formula 1's true home in America.

From its inaugural race in 2012, Austin felt like it could be the place where F1 finally laid down roots in the States. And over the years, the city and its Circuit of the Americas (COTA) have showed that it was not that F1 lacked appeal in the US, or that it could not make a success there. It was that for decades the sport was not doing the right things to generate that foothold.

Austin proved that, with the right circuit in the right place and the right management, F1 could be a success in the States. And the management part of it is where Taylor Swift comes in.

The US Grand Prix in Austin was an immediate hit when it made its debut in 2012. Austin might not be as famous as New York, San Francisco or Los Angeles, but it is a real gem.

Downtown and its environs buzz day and night. Live music is the heartbeat of the city, with bands playing from many bars, centred on Sixth Street but spilling into the surrounding areas and over the Colorado river on to trendy South Congress Avenue. The city is packed with interesting restaurant choices. The weather in October is usually warm and welcoming, and the city's atmosphere matches it.

Despite the race's instant popularity, crowds dropped slightly in each of the first three years, and the 2015 event – which was hit by heavy rain and high winds on the edge of a hurricane, which meant qualifying could not be run on Saturday – was "financially devastating for the company," according to Circuit of the Americas chairman Bobby Epstein.

The race had been born thanks to some clever financial thinking. It was commercially possible only because of the Texan major events reimbursement fund, a system by which event organisers can apply to have their expenses – everything from rights fees to employment costs – refunded by the state as long as they can establish that the event brings in at least that amount of money into the state from outside. The Grand Prix has always done so – in its first decade, it benefited the Texas economy to the tune of $10bn.

But in the wake of the 2015 losses, some more improvisation was required. Epstein, who had initially been only an investor in the race, took the reins: "I didn't actively run it until it was clear we were going the wrong way," he says.

"It was looking shaky as an event. What I noticed was that almost everyone they brought in to run it had racing backgrounds, or sports

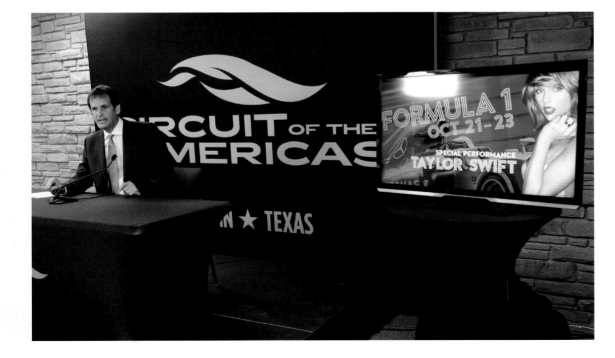

OPPOSITE: A view from Big Red down Phil Hill towards the start line. It has become regular practice for pole-sitters to push cars on the inside over the pit lane exit. Lewis Hamilton does the honours to Sebastian Vettel in 2017.

LEFT: A news agency photo of a 2016 Bobby Epstein press conference announcing the Taylor Swift concert amid what the picture caption references as COTA's 'financial struggles'.

backgrounds. And my role has always been from the beginning: what is the fan experience? The racing people focused more on execution and is the track right? But we don't really put on a race. Someone else does that. We just take care of the fans, and so I got more active, said I wanted to bring in a big music act, because F1 wasn't promoting the sport in the US."

It turned out that Swift's promoter lived in Austin. Epstein met him for lunch. "We were talking," Epstein recalls, "and he said: 'You know, Taylor Swift might do a show. She hasn't done a show because her mum's been ill and she has been spending time with her mother, but maybe you want to do a deal, make her an offer, be her only show of the year.'

"So we did, and Bernie said: 'Why should I even bring the cars, if you're just doing concerts?'"

The Taylor Swift concert in 2016 set the template for the US Grand Prix's continued success. The racing timetable was shifted later in the day, so fans could watch the action, and then the big concert would happen shortly afterwards, giving the race event wider appeal. It also kept tens of thousands of people at the track, raising extra money and spreading out the traffic, too. It was a triumph. Since Swift, many major global acts have played the US Grand Prix, including Elton John and the Rolling Stones.

Epstein's innovation has not only safeguarded one of the best races on the calendar. It has also provided a template for others to follow. And his foresight has secured an event that throughout the sport is one of the most popular of the year.

Austin's slogan is 'Keep Austin Weird'. But the city's 'weirdness' is rooted only in how

ABOVE: In Hermann Tilke's 'Best of' track, Turns 12 to 16 are a nod to the stadium section at Hockenheim.

different it is from the rest of Texas. A liberal stronghold in the middle of a state famous for its conservative politics, Austin is free-thinking and cosmopolitan. For a visitor from Europe, there is nothing weird about it at all.

The city is one side of the event's success. The other is the track. After Watkins Glen and Long Beach fell off the schedule, US Grands Prix were held at a series of unremarkable street circuits in places that had no connection with F1 – a car park at Caesars Palace in Las Vegas, Detroit, Dallas, Phoenix. None of them worked. F1 even seemed an odd fit at the road course inside the Indianapolis Motor Speedway.

But COTA, as Lewis Hamilton puts it, was an "instant classic". Max Verstappen calls the layout "amazing".

"This circuit is just incredible," Hamilton says. "It's one of the drivers' favourites, definitely one of my favourites. This is right up there with Silverstone. It really is a legendary layout that I think every driver finds really tricky. It's bumpy, incredibly challenging, each section."

Designed by F1's familiar track architect Hermann Tilke, who has been criticised for his uninspiring layouts at other venues, Tilke took the opportunity in Austin to design the layout he had always wanted to.

The land had varying topography. Epstein originally owned only the top half of the circuit, and had planned to build houses on it. But the 2008 financial crash nixed that. He was convinced by local businessmen to look into building a track, and it was Tilke who persuaded him to buy an adjacent plot that included a steep

hill, which became the signature steep rise up to Turn 1, now named 'Big Red' after one of the original investors, Red McCombs.

Esptein says: "We met with the Tilke organisation and they said: 'We have something we designed in the shop, so to speak, that we have not been able to do because most of the time the government gives us our land, we don't get any say-so in the topography and we've been given mainly flat land for the last x number of years.'"

It was Tilke who decided to do a kind of 'greatest hits of F1' layout, modelling the superlative Esses from Turns 3 to 6 on the Becketts complex at Silverstone, the 'stadium section' at the end of the long back straight on Hockenheim and the long right-hander towards the end of the lap on Turn 8 at Istanbul Park.

Epstein points out the campground behind Turn 1. "This grows every year," he says. "These are your best advocates. They tell their friends. If you hang out with someone for three days and

you are drinking coffee in the morning and beer at night it's: 'You coming back next year?' 'Yeah, I want to get spots next to you.'

"And these are the kinds of things that sustain and create history and tradition. It's one of the advantages of creating an event, whether it's Burning Man (festival) or anything else. There is a culture around it, that people want to be there and spend the whole weekend, and it's why some races are more than others."

Now, despite the advent of Miami and Las Vegas, Austin "feels like it has built up that identity of the American Grand Prix," according to multiple F1 winner Daniel Ricciardo. "It certainly feels very America out here and it's something that we've all enjoyed and got behind.

"The facility, the circuit, everything, the whole event is huge – 400,000 fans over the course of the weekend, or something like that. So not only us drivers but everyone loves it. It's a special thing."

LEFT: Carlos Sainz is edged sideways at the start of the 2023 grand prix as cars head off to the high-speed Silverstone-inspired esses.

BELOW: No need for the Lone Star state flag, the distinctive COTA tower tells us we're in Texas now.

Circuit Andorra

Port d'Envalira, Andorra

The highest Formula 1 circuit in the world is the Autódromo Hermanos Rodríguez in Mexico City. Its altitude of 2,238 metres (7,342 ft) is renowned for causing problems with reduced downforce and cooling for cars. But it's not the highest motor-racing circuit in the world. That honour goes to the Circuit Andorra in the Pyrenees.

Situated close to the village of Pas de la Casa and at the foot of the Grandvalira (or Grau Roig) ski resort, the Circuit Andorra is 2,400 metres (7,874 ft) above sea level. It is 29 kilometres (18 miles) – a drive of about 42 minutes in this terrain – east from the capital, Andorra la Vella. This tiny little track of just 945 metres (3,100 ft) in length – so short that the starting grid takes up a third of the entire circuit – features seven corners, and is in the most enviable location surrounded by jagged mountain peaks.

The circuit is in operation year round. Members of the public can go there in the summer to try out go-karts or motorbikes, or take road-safety courses. Or in the winter to learn about ice-driving. This can be either with vehicles supplied by the track or even in your own car.

But the track has been the venue for two different winter motorsport events – the G Series for buggy-style vehicles and most famously a round of the Trophée Andros, France's national ice racing series.

Over the years, this has attracted a multitude of famous racing drivers, including four-time Formula 1 world champion Alain Prost, who took three championship titles and 38 race wins between 1987 and 2001. Incongruously, one of the most successful grand prix drivers of all time won his final crown in 2011, at the age of 56 – in a Dacia.

Established in 1990, the Trophée Andros started at Serre Chevalier in the Hautes-Alpes. The Andorra race, first held in 2005–6, was the only round not held in France, apart from when the series went to Canada, to Sherbrooke in Quebec, for three seasons. For many years, the Andros championship was for petrol cars but after introducing electric cars in 2009, it made the full switch to only electric vehicles for the 2019–20 season.

But at a time when the climate crisis is an increasing concern globally, and F1 is aiming to be net-zero by 2030 with the use of sustainable fuels, the Trophée Andros provides a stark reminder of what's at stake, and the existential risk global warming poses to motorsport.

Its final season was the 2023–24 series, and it was cancelled because organisers were finding it increasingly difficult to find the required snowy and icy conditions in France. Or even at 2,400 metres (7,874 ft) in the Andorran Pyrenees.

OPPOSITE: French driver Gérald Fontanel in a Nice Metropole Renault Zoe competing in the 2019 eTrophée Andros.

BELOW LEFT: Even at a 2,400-metre (7,874-ft) altitude, it's a struggle to keep the circuit icy.

BELOW: Former French F1 driver Olivier Panis (like Alain Prost) is also an ice racer, along with his son Aurélien.

Circuit de Charade

Saint-Gènes-Champanelle, France

The Circuit du Charade, in France's Auvergne region just outside Clermont-Ferrand, is primarily famous for two reasons. It was the track where Helmut Marko lost his left eye, forcing his retirement from racing, and where a great driver renowned for terrible bad luck suffered a day that summed up his entire career.

Both these events happened in the same race, the 1972 French Grand Prix. It was also the last time Formula 1 cars raced on a track that arguably was the best France ever had. The original Charade circuit ran for just over 8km (5 miles), with 48 corners, in the shadow of the Puy de Dôme, perhaps the most famous of the extinct volcanoes that make up the Massif Central.

The volcanic landscape both made the circuit and signed its death warrant. The track was renowned for its extreme challenge — likened by many to an even faster version of the famous Nürburgring Nordschleife — but also the volcanic stones that lined the track.

Cars that ran wide would flick these stones onto the track surface, and it was one of them, sent flying by Ronnie Peterson's March, that pierced the visor of Marko's helmet and blinded him in his left eye. It forced the end of the career of a man who, not long before, had set a lap record on the Targa Florio that stands to this day, who had won Le Mans the year before, and was just beginning to make his name in F1.

Meanwhile, at the front of the race, Chris Amon was dominating in his Matra until he, too, fell

foul of the stones. He was one of 10 drivers to suffer a puncture that day, and he was forced into the pits to change it. This handed the win to Jackie Stewart and led to a stunning comeback drive from Amon, who shattered the lap record on his recovery to third place. Amon, regarded as one of the fastest and most talented drivers of his era, was never to win a grand prix. But this drive showed what an injustice that statistic was.

It was the sort of place where the greatest shone. Of the four French Grands Prix held there, Jim Clark won one, Stewart two, and Jochen Rindt the other. The pole positions were taken by Clark, Rindt, Jacky Ickx and Amon. In 1965, on the way to one of six consecutive victories that year in his Lotus-Climax, Clark was 3 seconds up on the rest of the field after one lap; six after two. After that, the win was not in doubt, as indeed it hardly ever was that year, the second of the Scot's two world championship seasons.

But after 1972, the track was deemed too dangerous, and the grand prix moved away. Eventually it was deemed too dangerous even for slower, national races, and a shorter 3.97km (2.47 mile) track was opened, using only the southern portion of the old track and removing the magnificent eastern loop.

These days, it hosts driving courses, track days and historic motorsport events — but the original parts of the classic track can still be enjoyed, up to a point — they are still in use as public roadways.

OPPOSITE: The circles to the right of the track mark the starting spots for drivers' 'Le Mans' starts. This GT sportscar race is from 1962, four years before director John Frankenheimer's camera arrived to record the French GP for his epic film.

BELOW: The local commune has worked hard to preserve elements of the old track and keep the memories of this classic circuit alive.

Circuit de Monaco

Monte Carlo, Monaco

The Monaco Grand Prix is the very essence of Formula 1. It's where sport collides with money; old money with new money; history with modernity. And it's where a drivers' task in not colliding with the barriers is harder than anywhere else on the calendar.

Monaco starts with the setting – an enclave on the glamorous Côte d'Azur surrounded by cliffs, blue Mediterranean skies, water sparkling – it could hardly be more evocative. For the most part, the city clings to the cliff face, and the track winds through it, up the hill and down again before circumnavigating the harbour, packed with boats, big and small – increasingly big, in fact, as the years have gone by.

The circuit is just 3.34km (2.07 miles) long, and its average speed is so slow that it is the only race that does not run to the full mandated 305km (190 mile) grand prix distance, because doing so would take it beyond the maximum permitted two-hour time limit.

But speed is relative when you are threading an aircraft-with-wheels between metal barriers, and Monaco packs a whole lot into the shortest lap on the F1 calendar.

OPPOSITE: In 1957, the start-finish straight was just about where the pit lane is today. Tony Brooks (20) in the Vanwall and Mike Hawthorn (28) in the Lancia-Ferrari round the Gasworks Hairpin.

BELOW LEFT: Massenet corner, approaching Casino Square, is little changed since the 1930s.

BELOW: The Monaco Grand Prix was promoted with classic posters from 'Geo Ham', Georges Hammel, who designed artwork for the race from the 1930s to the 1950s.

This would be a great track even without its setting, a "ten out of ten", as Daniel Ricciardo describes it. Corner after corner, inclines, blind entries, no room for error with barriers lining the entire track, threading the needle. But the location amplifies it exponentially.

The grand prix was first held in 1929, and quickly made its name in the era of F. Scott Fitzgerald and W. Somerset Maugham, whose description of this area as 'a sunny place for shady people' has stuck with good reason. Monaco has long been a place where people with a lot of money, whether earned respectably or not, have come to hide it away from the tax regimes of their home countries.

Along the coast, many of the bijou towns are still recognizably as Fitzgerald described in his novel *Tender is the Night*. But in Monaco, the Belle

Epoque villas are increasingly being crowded out by modern apartment buildings. As elegance is replaced by brash ostentation, the romance of the place has undoubtedly declined. But as a location to host a grand prix, to attract the great and good, all keen to bask in its golden glamour glow, its charisma is undimmed.

If Monaco has changed quite a bit since the race was first held there, the track itself has not. The Monaco Grand Prix circuit has essentially had only one major modification to it in the past century. The fact that today's stars are still driving on the same track as did the first winner, William Grover-Williams, or Achille Varzi, Juan Manuel Fangio and Stirling Moss, is part of its enduring appeal.

The section from the start-finish line, through Sainte Dévote, up the hill, over the crest into

the fast Massenet left-hander, which leads into Casino Square, down to Mirabeau, the hotel hairpin, and Portier out along the sea front through the tunnel, is essentially the same as it has always been.

The harbour-front (Nouvelle) chicane, previously a very fast left-right flick, was slowed down in 1986 for safety reasons. But it is the section after Tabac, the quick left-hander after the chicane on the corner of the harbour, that has changed most.

Until 1972, there was a straight after Tabac all the way to the old Gasworks hairpin, which directed the cars back up the start-finish straight. It was here that Jack Brabham, under increasing pressure from the Lotus of Jochen Rindt, crashed on the last lap in 1970, handing victory to his rival, starting the cascade of wins that were to lead to the Austrian becoming the sport's only posthumous world champion.

For 1973, a double chicane had to be inserted along the harbour front as the track navigated around a new swimming pool. The change made overtaking harder, but introduced perhaps the best corner on the whole track – the high-speed first left-right into the Swimming Pool section is one of the most awe-inspiring places to watch F1 cars first hand on the whole calendar.

The Swimming Pool corners have been tempered since they were first built. For a couple of decades, the apexes of the first chicane were concrete walls. Now, the wall has been moved backwards and low kerbs mark the limits of the track. Even so, the speed of the cars and the precision of their drivers as they thread through the narrow confines here are mind-boggling, and bring to mind Jenson Button's comment about Monaco: "It's madness driving around here," he said. "In a good way."

The cars have changed the experience of Monaco as much as anything. Until the late

1970s, the place to watch was at the top of the hill at Casino Square, on the outside of the track at the exit of the corner. This was quintessential Monaco. In front, the lavish rococo towers of the Casino. To the right, the Hotel de Paris, the principality's most famous hotel, where the winner's ball is held on the Sunday evening, and where Jackie Stewart, a three-time winner, still stays every year, half a century since he retired.

Here, as the cars exited the right-hander, the crest of the road would flick them sideways, the driver fighting to retain control. The image of a car at 30 degrees or more, a grand Riviera hotel in the background; that was Monaco in a single frame.

But the advent of aerodynamics has meant the drivers have to keep their cars straight, to retain that all-important optimum airflow. And that means the real eye-popping places to watch are now different.

OPPOSITE: Lorenzo Bandini's Ferrari 156 in Casino Square – park benches and all – on his way to third place in the 1962 race.

LEFT: Gilles Villeneuve performs miracles with his 'big red Cadillac' in the 1981 race.

BELOW: Riccardo Patrese, the accidental winner in 1982.

Nothing quite matches the Swimming Pool complex, but for sensory overload it's tough to beat the tunnel. Standing behind the barrier as the cars scream past, you feel an F1 car as much as see it. The violence is overwhelming, with the force of the air displaced by a car moving at 290km/h (180mph) pushing you backwards.

Massenet, the long left-hander before Casino Square, is another classic – the car goes light over a crest just before entry and it's all too easy to misjudge it and slide into the wall (as Fernando Alonso found out in 2010). Overall, the track is a challenge like no other. In the decade from 1984 to 1993, only two drivers won here, and they were the two best in the world at the time, Ayrton Senna and Alain Prost.

Taking an F1 car through these streets, between the barriers, requires a mental adjustment even for those who have done it many times before. "Just getting out on track is always a big shock in just how fast everything is," says Lewis Hamilton, who won at Monaco in 2008, 2016 and 2019.

Monaco is a track that needs to be built up to – even for the very best. The climax of the weekend is in many ways qualifying, when the drivers take their cars and themselves to the limit for the only time. A contender for the all-time greatest lap around Monaco has to be the one that put Gilles Villeneuve on the front row in his Ferrari 126C in 1981. The car that beat him to pole – Nelson Piquet's Brabham BT49 – is now known to have been running underweight – its rear wing was swapped for a heavier one by its mechanics after the session, to ensure it complied with the minimum limit.

Villeneuve's car had prodigious power from its turbo engine, but was ill-suited for a track that is essentially all corners, with a chassis that was among the worst in the field, and which he laughingly called his "big red Cadillac".

Yet, extraordinarily, the Canadian was just 0.078 seconds off pole. His teammate Didier Pironi could manage only 17th, 2.5 seconds off Villeneuve's pace.

That qualifying lap was the foundation for one of Monaco's most unlikely victories. In the race, Villeneuve's cumbersome Ferrari could not keep up with Piquet, and was passed early on by the similarly nimble Williams of Alan Jones and Arrows of Riccardo Patrese. But Piquet crashed while under pressure from Jones, and Patrese retired, and when Jones ran into fuel-pressure trouble late in the race, Villeneuve was still close enough to catch the Williams, and swoop by for the win.

A year later, Monaco was the first race held after Villeneuve crashed to his death in qualifying for the Belgian Grand Prix, and it staged arguably its most madcap event. Pole-sitter René Arnoux crashed his Renault at the Swimming Pool after 14 laps, handing the lead to his teammate Prost, who led most of the rest of the way. But when a shower hit the track late on, Prost crashed at the chicane, and soon it began to look like a race no one wanted to win. Patrese inherited the lead, only to spin himself on oil at the hotel hairpin with a lap and a half to go.

That put Pironi's Ferrari in front, but his car broke down in the tunnel on the final lap. Andrea de Cesaris's Alfa Romeo ran out of fuel before the Italian could pass Pironi. The gearbox in Derek Daly's Williams seized before he started the final lap. And through the chaos came Patrese, who had managed to bump-start his car on the hill down to Portier. He crossed the line for his maiden victory – and had no idea he was the winner as he did so.

Over the years, Monaco has seen it all, from virtuoso driving performances, to madcap races, to tragedy, to naked cheating. Michael Schumacher ties with Graham Hill as the second most successful driver ever around the streets with five wins, behind only Senna with six, but the great German's name will forever be associated with one of the most outrageous pieces of underhand behaviour in F1 history.

In qualifying for the 2006 race, Schumacher was running ahead of his title rival Fernando Alonso as they embarked on their final lap. Schumacher was on provisional pole, having been faster on their first runs, but after two of three sectors, Alonso was 0.2 seconds up on the Ferrari driver's time, and thus on course to wrest the ideal starting position from his title rival.

But then Schumacher drove slowly into the barriers on the exit of Rascasse corner, stopping against the wall but not damaging his car, and preventing Alonso from completing his lap.

And there was uproar. It was perhaps the most egregious example of a recurring character flaw of Schumacher's – the instinct, when in moments of the most extreme pressure, to go for the low blow. The 1982 world champion Keke Rosberg called it, "the cheapest, dirtiest thing I have ever seen in F1". Schumacher was disqualified and sent to the back of the grid.

He has never admitted his guilt. Even when he retired for the second time after his ill-fated return to Formula 1 with Mercedes, the closest he came to expressing regret was to say: "We are all humans and we all make mistakes and with hindsight you would probably do it differently if you had a second opportunity, but that's life".

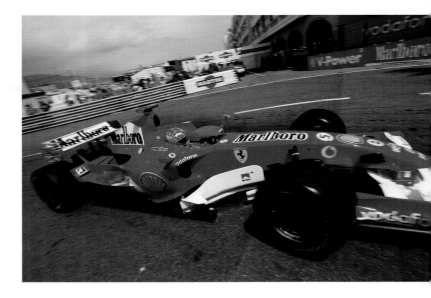

ABOVE: Schumacher approaches Rascasse in 2006.

RIGHT: Alonso threads the needle through the Swimming Pool complex in 2023. The common accident is turning in a fraction early and hitting the barrier with the front right of the car.

OPPOSITE RIGHT: Max Verstappen has had two major shunts at the exit of the Swimming Pool, this one is from 2016.

OPPOSITE LEFT: Mick Schumacher signals to the marshal that he is okay, but this 2022 shunt at the Swimming Pool cost Haas close to a million dollars.

As for tragedy, Monaco was the scene of one of the worst examples of the lack of safety in the late 1960s, the culmination of which persuaded Stewart to embark on the campaign that forever changed the face of F1.

In 1967, Lorenzo Bandini crashed his Ferrari at the chicane while trying to catch the leader Denny Hulme's McLaren. The Italian's car came to rest upside down and on fire but the race was not stopped. Passing cars hindered the rescue efforts, and none of the marshals present had fire-proof clothes. Bandini was in the burning car for five minutes, and died in hospital three days later.

Shocking and unforgivable tragedy notwithstanding, perhaps the Monaco moment that resonates most strongly through history involves Senna. His pole lap in 1988, his first year with McLaren-Honda, has gone down in legend. The McLaren MP4/4 was in a league of its own that year, but, around Monaco, Senna took his car and himself into uncharted territory with a lap that was 1.457 seconds quicker than teammate Alain Prost.

Later, in an interview with the Canadian journalist Gerald Donaldson, Senna described a kind of out-of-body experience as he circulated Monaco that day.

"Suddenly I realised I was no longer driving the car consciously," he said. "I was driving it by a kind of instinct, only I was in a different dimension. It was like I was in a tunnel. I was way over the limit but still able to find even more. It frightened me because I was well beyond my conscious understanding."

Monaco has a unique magic to it, and few moments there have ever been more magical than that.

OPPOSITE ABOVE: The Nouvelle Chicane has been tightened over the years to slow cars down as they approach the harbour front.

OPPOSITE BELOW: Drivers have to be watchful for opportunist overtaking moves into the Old Station Hairpin on the opening lap. In 2019 Daniel Ricciardo (4) puts a move on Charles Leclerc (16).

BELOW: The run from Mirabeau to the Fairmont Hotel Hairpin, a corner that has had many names over the years. It started life as the Station Hairpin – the old station was demolished to build Loews Hotel, which was renamed the Grand Hotel and has now become Fairmont Monte Carlo.

Circuit de Spa-Francorchamps

Francorchamps, Belgium

For a century, racing drivers have had a love-hate relationship with the Spa-Francorchamps circuit in Belgium. In recent decades, it has been mostly love, tempered with wariness and respect for the risks they know they are taking at one of the fastest and most demanding tracks in the world. Particularly if the weather turns, as it so often does in this corner of the Ardennes forest.

Before the modern, shortened version of Spa was created at 7.00km (4.35 miles) in length, the original track took drivers on a 14.5km

(9 mile) triangular blast through the hills, where the predominant emotion was fear.

Take Jim Clark as an example. He was the preeminent driver of the 1960s, the man every one of his contemporaries accepted as the best — and is someone who is still regularly near the top of many people's lists of the greatest grand prix drivers of all time — and he mastered Spa like few others before or since.

Clark won the Belgian Grand Prix for four consecutive years from 1962 to 1965. One of

them was a performance for the ages — in 1963, in teaming rain, the Scot's Lotus lapped the entire field except for Bruce McLaren's Cooper, and won by almost five minutes. And yet Clark hated Spa.

Why? Because he had seen first hand, too many times, what it could do. In Clark's very first Belgian Grand Prix, in 1960, his teammate Alan Stacey was killed when a bird hit him in the face. A few minutes later at the same corner, Burnenville, fellow Briton Chris Bristow lost control right in front of Clark and was thrown into barbed wire and decapitated.

These accidents happened just 24 hours after Stirling Moss, the man whose mantle as greatest driver in the world Clark was poised to inherit, was himself badly injured in a crash in practice, also at Burnenville; a fast, banked, downhill right-hander that led on to the straight that contained the most fearsome corner on the track, the Masta Kink. Another driver, Mike Taylor, was also severely injured here in an accident in which he was flung into a tree.

Spa was built in 1921 when Jules de Thier, the owner of a newspaper in the nearby town of

OPPOSITE: Alberto Ascari takes the chequered flag in his Ferrari. There were only six F1 championship races in 1952, but Ascari won all of them. Just visible beyond the driver's helmet is the prominent half-timbered building on the outside of La Source.

LEFT: The start of the grand prix in 1964, when the starting grid was positioned after La Source Hairpin, with cars facing downhill towards Eau Rouge.

Liège, decided, along with two friends, that the roads from Francorchamps through the towns of Burnenville, Malmedy and Stavelot would form an ideal circuit with very few slow corners and lots of fast, demanding sections. It held its first grand prix in 1925.

Spa was one of many classic tracks that were born in the 1920s, that era of optimism and possibility that preceded the stock market crash of 1929, the rise of fascism and the descent into world war. The Nürburgring, not far away across the German border in the same range of hills, was another. For all of Nürburgring's fearsome reputation, it was Spa that the drivers were most apprehensive about.

At the very beginning, the corner for which Spa has since become famous – the fast swerves known globally as Eau Rouge – was not part of the track. Instead, where there is now a fast left into a compression and then a precipitous rise uphill through a right and then a left over a crest, the track turned sharp left to a hairpin named for the old customs house that was situated there: the Virage de l'Ancienne Douane.

The hairpin was bypassed and Eau Rouge added in 1939, with the aim of making the track even faster. That year, the track claimed its first big name when Richard 'Dick' Seaman crashed his Mercedes into a tree while leading the race in treacherous wet conditions.

That was the thing about Spa. Until 1970, there were no barriers. If you went off, you didn't know what you were going to hit. A tree, a house, perhaps a ditch or a fence.

No corner was more notorious than the Masta Kink, a left-right between houses, that Jackie Stewart called "by far the most difficult corner in the world". Masta, which bisected a long straight between Burnenville and Stavelot, was fast, very fast, but back in the 1960s not quite flat out.

ABOVE: Cars climb the hill from Eau Rouge towards Raidillon in 1970, the final year before the grand prix was cancelled on safety grounds. The white dotted line shows that Eau Rouge was still in use as a public road.

The challenge was to take it as quickly as possible while maximising the exit, because the tiniest miscalculation meant a drop in speed that would cost the driver lap time all the way to the next corner at Stavelot.

As the 1960s progressed, time was clearly running out on the track, and the 1966 race was the beginning of the end for the original Spa. Stewart crashed at the Masta Kink, hit a telegraph pole and ended up trapped upside down in his BRM in a farmyard, fuel leaking around him.

Stewart was stuck there for nearly half an hour, and was rescued only when fellow drivers Graham Hill and Bob Bondurant, both of whom had gone off nearby, managed to extricate him with the help of a spectator's toolkit.

There were no doctors or medical facilities, and Stewart was placed on the back of a pick-up truck until an ambulance arrived. That took him to the circuit medical centre, where he was left

on a stretcher on the floor amid cigarette ends and other rubbish, before another ambulance picked him up to take him to hospital in Liège, only to get lost on the way.

After that, Stewart became a passionate advocate for improving safety; he led a boycott of the 1969 Grand Prix at Spa. The last grand prix at the old circuit was in 1970, when BRM's Pedro Rodríguez managed to hold off the faster Ferrari of Chris Amon by just over a second after a long, tense slipstreaming battle, the extra straight-line speed of the BRM just winning out over the Ferrari's better handling.

Although the old track was now an anachronism, local officials were determined to attract F1 back to the region, and in 1979 the track was shortened. The area around the pits and down through Eau Rouge was left intact, but the new layout turned right at Les Combes where the old had gone left, and introduced a new section that swept downhill through a series of swerves

TOP LEFT: When the grand prix reconvened in 1983, the pit buildings were now in their current location and the starting grid had moved to before La Source – though still a public road.

TOP RIGHT: Jim Clark, photographed in his Lotus 25 at Spa in 1962.

ABOVE: In the chaotic 1998 race, Michael Schumacher turned his Ferrari into a three-wheeler when he clattered into the back of David Coulthard's McLaren, trying to lap the Scot.

before rejoining the old track on the run down to the flat-out Blanchimont left-hander.

F1 returned to Spa in 1983, and the Belgian Grand Prix has stayed there ever since, apart from a one-off return to Zolder in 1984. It has held many classics since, such as 1998, when eleven cars crashed in the mist after La Source on the first lap, and then Michael Schumacher

tried to throttle David Coulthard after running his Ferrari into the back of his McLaren while leading the race. Or 2000, when Mika Häkkinen chased down Schumacher on a drying track and pulled off one of the greatest overtaking moves of all time, the two spearing either side of a shocked back marker as Häkkinen claimed the lead, a lap after Schumacher had edged him towards the grass at 322km/h (200mph) at the same spot.

The modification of the circuit was a masterpiece in sensitive redesign, keeping the high-speed, flowing character of the old track but updating it for a modern age. And it introduced another magnificent corner in the long, downhill double left-hander known as Pouhon. Nowadays, when aerodynamic downforce has made Eau Rouge 'easy flat' in an F1 car, at least in the dry, Pouhon has become

Spa's most demanding corner. But the whole track has a beautiful, organic flow as it rises and falls around the landscape, of which it feels a part. It is, as Mark Webber once said, a lap "that makes you feel like you're going somewhere". Or as former F1 driver Romain Grosjean put it: "It is a circuit with a soul."

Until 2000, the run from La Source hairpin, the first corner, through Eau Rouge up to Les Combes was a public highway – vehicles going south would take the swerves; those going north were sent right to the old custom house hairpin. But from 2001 the whole track was closed off and became a permanent circuit. Its layout, though, was unchanged, save for a tweak at the final chicane, which was turned from a 'Bus Stop', left-right, right-left, into a clumsy and tight right-left, the only 'bad' corner on the track.

Spa might be modernized and updated, but its forbidding nature remains. Like Suzuka, if you go off at Spa, you will likely hit something. Not a tree or a house any more, but a barrier. And as the track is so fast, you will hit it hard. Nowhere more so than at Eau Rouge.

Eau Rouge is actually the shorthand name for two corners. Officially, it is Eau Rouge-Raidillon. Eau Rouge is the name of the stream that runs under the track, and which gives its name to the first, left-handed part of the swerves into the compression at the bottom of the hill after the long descent from La Source. The steep climb up the other side, through the fast right-hander and then over the crest as the track turns left, that is all Raidillon – literally, small, steep road.

OPPOSITE: The grandstand facing Eau Rouge and the old start-finish straight was massively enlarged in 2022.

ABOVE RIGHT: Rubens Barrichello driving for the 'Mayfly' Brawn team rounds La Source Hairpin in 2009.

RIGHT: The run up to Les Combes is often a slipstreaming battle and often it's best to be second out of La Source.

In an F1 car in qualifying trim in the dry, this section of the track is taken flat out without a lift of the throttle. But the compression and sheer speed – entry at close to 322km/h (200mph) – means it remains a significant challenge. As Mercedes F1 team principal Toto Wolff puts it: "If you drive towards Eau Rouge at 260–270km/h, which looks like a 90-degree corner, and you take it flat, it is beyond understanding that these guys do what they do."

In the wet, or with a full tank of fuel, Eau Rouge still requires throttle modulation. But flat out or not, the danger remains. If anything goes wrong here, the walls are close, even after the most recent safety changes. And arguably the most dangerous section is actually after the corner,

once the cars have crested the rise, and up on to the Kemmel Straight.

The problem is that the topography of the landscape means there is only so much room for safety features, and because of the high speeds involved, cars that go off tend to bounce back on to the track, where they can be hit by other cars, which are still travelling at very high speeds.

This is what happened in the accident that killed Formula 2 driver Anthoine Hubert on the exit of Raidillon at the 2019 Belgian Grand Prix, and the crash that took the life of Dutch Formula 4 driver Dilano Van 't Hoff, a little further along the straight, in July 2023. In Van t' Hoff's case, poor visibility because of heavy rain – a regular

occurrence in the Ardennes forest – made the accident more likely.

Spa therefore confronts racing drivers in a very visceral and immediate sense with the dangers of the profession they chose because they love it. They know what they do is dangerous, and they compartmentalise that risk most of the time. But driving at Spa forces them to face the fact that the possibility of paying the ultimate price is an inherent part of that love. It goes without saying that the the drivers don't want to be injured, or worse, but the very fact they can be adds an extra frisson to what they do, and Spa is the sort of place where the intoxication and contradiction inherent in that mix is at its very highest.

Daniel Ricciardo admitted that Hubert's accident forced him to deliberate on why he does what he does for a living. "You question, 'Is it really worth it?' for sure, because at the end of the day, it's a simple question but it's a pretty honest one as well," he said.

"Yeah, it's our job and it's our profession and it's our life, but also it's still just racing cars around in circles."

The drivers nearly always conclude that it is worth it, though. "I can't explain that," Ricciardo says. "It's probably just when you have a deep passion and love for something. It is still in your mind, of course. But we're able to put it to one side for a moment."

In the end, the joy that drivers get from Spa supersedes the risks of driving it. As Lewis Hamilton puts it; "everyone has a special feeling with Spa".

For Max Verstappen, it's his "favourite track". But even he admits: "It is amazing to drive in the dry, and when you then have a wet qualifying, it's pretty.... I wouldn't say scary but it's really interesting and quite extreme."

Or, to put it the way Wolff does, Spa is a reminder of a simple truth about motorsport. "It is still a gladiators' sport," he says.

OPPOSITE: Looking down on the final chicane – previously the Bus Stop Chicane – before the start-finish straight.

TOP: La Source Hairpin has been witness to some spectacular accidents over the years, with Fernando Alonso's McLaren getting launched over Charles Leclerc's Sauber in 2018.

LEFT: Rain is never far away from the forests of the Ardennes and in 2021 spectators had to endure a will they/won't they start to the race for four hours. They never did start it.

Circuit Gilles Villeneuve

Montréal, Canada

The Canadian Grand Prix is one of Formula 1's classic races – and it is held on a charismatic track named after an iconic driver whose light shone bright and brief and who is still worshipped more than 40 years after his untimely death.

Gilles Villeneuve was a son of Quebec, born in Berthierville, about 40km (25 miles) south-west of Montréal. And when he took his maiden F1 victory at the wheel of a Ferrari 312T3 at the 1978 Canadian Grand Prix, at the inaugural race for a new street circuit held on the city's Île Notre-Dame, a national hero was born.

Villeneuve was somewhat lucky to win that chilly October day – he inherited the lead thanks to the retirement of the Lotus of Jean-Pierre Jarier,

a replacement for Swede Ronnie Peterson, killed in a crash at Monza a month before.

But the young driver's talent was already well known. Enzo Ferrari had signed him up after only one race – a spectacular debut in an outdated McLaren at Silverstone in 1977. Villeneuve's first full season had been full of promise, and that day in Montréal the other drivers he beat to stand on top of the podium underlined the quality of his drive. Second was Jody Scheckter, who was moving to Ferrari to be Villeneuve's teammate the following season, and third was Villeneuve's current teammate, Carlos Reutemann. Great drivers both.

A year later, Villeneuve cemented his legend with the home fans. Scheckter had already

been crowned world champion at the wheel of Ferrari's 312T4 car – a status Villeneuve was unlucky not to earn for himself – but it was the Canadian who took the fight for victory in Montréal to the faster Williams FW07 of Alan Jones, the form combination of the second half of 1979. Villeneuve held off Jones for most of the race before the Australian finally found a way by. But still he could not shake the Ferrari; Villeneuve crossed the line just a second behind.

OPPOSITE: Lewis Hamilton exits Turn 2 at the 2023 Canadian Grand Prix.

BELOW LEFT: Gilles's wife, Joann, with their son (right) at the re-dedication of the memorial line in 2018. Each decade anniversary of his 1978 victory is marked with a new inscription.

BELOW: Gilles Villeneuve pictured in 1981.

Gilles was to have only two further home races before he was killed in a crash during qualifying for the 1982 Belgian GP. By that time he had established himself as the fastest driver in the world, and a fan favourite. The Circuit Île Notre-Dame was re-named for him by the time F1 returned for the race a month after his death.

In a horrible, tragic twist, Villeneuve's teammate, Didier Pironi, was on pole that day, and dedicated it to his late rival. However, the Frenchman stalled at the start, and he was hit with sickening force by the Osella of novice Riccardo Paletti, who had qualified 23rd and was doing well over 161km/h (100mph) when he slammed, unsighted, into the back of the Ferrari. The Italian became the second fatality of one of F1's most awful seasons.

Villeneuve is revered as one of the most exciting, attacking drivers F1 has ever seen. Fortunately, the Circuit Gilles Villeneuve – which, soon after his death, had the legend 'Salut Gilles' painted

on the grid – is a fitting tribute. It's hardly the Nürburgring Nordschleife, but a layout that looks deceptively simple from the track map – a 4.36km (2.70 mile) track on a man-made island made up largely of straights and a series of chicanes – is actually anything but.

The walls are close, the surface is low-grip, braking into the slow corners from high speeds is a test of judgement, and there are some deceptive camber changes that add to the difficulty. Brake wear is often a problem.

A measure of the test the track provides for the drivers is that two in particular have mastered it over the years – and they are the two most successful of all time. Michael Schumacher and Lewis Hamilton have each won there seven times, their improvisational skills well suited to the skittish circuit. No one else has more than three victories.

In Villeneuve's day, and until 1995, the track had two more corners than it does today – the

OPPOSITE: Alain Prost rounds the hairpin in his Ferrari in 1991 with the Biosphere and downtown Montreal as a backdrop.

BELOW LEFT: Robert Kubica's BMW Sauber is pitched into a roll after tangling with Jarno Trulli in 2007. Kubica was unhurt and wanted to start the United States GP in Indianapolis a week later.

BELOW: Charles Leclerc keeps it on the island as he passes the Casino de Montréal, the French pavilion at the 1967 Expo.

BOTTOM: The Alpine of Esteban Ocon rejoins the race in 2022. The pit lane exit was modified for 2002, emerging safely beyond Turn 1.

long straight running from the hairpin to the final chicane used to have a high-speed left-right S-bend in the middle, called Casino. It was removed for the 1996 race on safety grounds, but while that deprived the track of perhaps its best corner, the essential character of the track remained, and if anything the changes heightened the challenge of the final chicane.

It meant the speeds from which drivers were braking for it were higher, which made it more difficult to judge the entry. Get it only slightly wrong and the result was to bounce over the kerbs of the second, left-handed part and lose control, with the outside wall waiting right on the track edge.

It was after this change to the track that the wall on the exit of that chicane earned its modern nickname. It became the 'Wall of Champions' at the 1999 Grand Prix, when Damon Hill, Schumacher and Jacques Villeneuve, Gilles's son, all crashed there.

The wall has continued to claim victims in the succeeding years – Sebastian Vettel added to the list of former champions to crunch his car against it in practice in 2011, the year Jenson Button took an extraordinary victory in a rain-hit race that ran to more than four hours. The McLaren driver had been last of all at half-distance, made six trips down the pit lane, and took the lead only halfway around the final lap,

when an under-pressure Vettel got slightly off line on a drying track and half spun.

To add to the atmosphere at the Circuit Gilles Villeneuve, it is a picturesque place. The buildings created for the 1967 Expo, including the Biosphere, which can be seen from the hairpin, and the aforementioned casino add colour amid the verdant backdrop. The skyline of buzzy, cosmopolitan downtown Montréal, a beguiling blend of European and North American influences, is just across the St Lawrence Seaway from the circuit, and the mighty river itself, broad and cold and forbidding, provides a metaphor for the existential risks drivers are taking every time they climb into their racing cars.

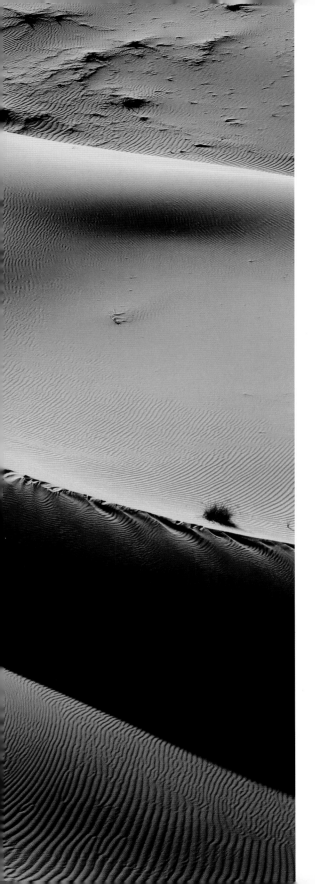

Dakar Rally

Al-Ula to Yanbu, Saudi Arabia

Jacky Ickx is a driver with a fair few accolades: he won eight grands prix titles; came second in the Formula 1 world championship with Ferrari in 1970; took three F1 pole positions and one victory at the Nürburgring Nordschleife; is the second most successful driver in the history of Le Mans (with six victories); and has a Bathurst 1000 to his name. But, for him, "the most difficult race on the planet" is the Dakar Rally.

Ickx won the Dakar in 1983 in a Mercedes. He was also the driving force behind Porsche entering the rally in the mid-1980s, and finished second for them in 1986 and then for Peugeot in 1989. The Belgian says this marathon rally raid across vast expanses of desert is a voyage of philosophical discovery as much as a competition between drivers and their machines.

"In the desert," Ickx says, "where you cannot cheat, you are facing the reality of what is a human being on this planet. You see people are living in it and it forces you to open your eyes to what is around you. You discover your value. You are facing the short amount of time you are here. You are existing in the global life of this incredible earth you are on. It is a big step.

"After Dakar, I realised I was not alone on the planet of motor racing. It helped me a lot to consider those who make all these things possible. I am what I am by these anonymous people; 90% of the iceberg is them. I am the mirror of those people. Respect. Respect for those who made it possible. And their expertise and know-how and wish to do perfection."

The Paris-Dakar, as it was known when it was inaugurated in 1977, was the brainchild of a Frenchman called Thierry Sabine, a bearded, iconoclastic visionary with a penchant for wearing sandals and a white jumpsuit. He was in the mould of his countrymen who dreamt up so much of modern sport in the early part of the 20th century.

OPPOSITE: Qatari driver Nasser Al-Attiyah takes his own route through the Saudi dunes on Stage 6 in 2024.

BELOW: Jacky Ickx contemplates the task in front of him in the 1986 Paris-Dakar Rally. Ickx came second in his Porsche 959, but the event was overshadowed by the death of organiser Thierry Sabine in a helicopter crash.

The Dakar follows in the grand tradition of the Fifa World Cup, the Tour de France and Le Mans 24 Hours. A big idea that captures the imagination and generates its own spirit and image; its cachet the romanticism of racing cars, bikes and trucks across the Sahara, driving blind, with only a map to guide you from the starting point of a day's stage to the end.

Seventy-four vehicles started the first event in 1977. By 1983, there were nearly 400 entrants, and his experience that year gave Ickx an idea. Driving for Porsche in endurance racing at the time, he saw the marketing possibilities and, on his return to Europe, convinced the German marque's bosses to prepare a car for the event.

Ickx had good timing. Porsche was in the process of developing its first four-wheel drive transmission, and recognized the benefits competing on the Dakar could bring. Porsche won on its debut in 1984, with Frenchman René Metge driving a heavily modified four-wheel

drive 911. Two years later, now using a modified 959 – a high-tech, four-wheel drive supercar then competing with Ferrari's stripped-out F40 for the honour of being the world's fastest and most glamorous car – Metge won again, Ickx following him across the line to make it a one-two.

By now, the Dakar had fully established itself as one of the high points of the motorsport calendar. The sense of genuine adventure, and the visceral immensity of the challenge, had captured imaginations around the world. It's quite possible that the current enthusiasm for SUVs among road car buyers had its first seeds in the success of the Dakar Rally. Ickx certainly thinks so.

In 1986, though, the event had its first major blow. In a chaotic edition, chronicled by some of the world's leading media outlets, drawn by the obvious potential for a story, Thierry Sabine was killed when his helicopter crashed in a

sandstorm in Mali, some 322km (200 miles) east of Timbuktu. French singer Daniel Balavoine – who had been invited to the rally by Sabine in the hope that fundraising for water wells in Africa could benefit from the Dakar's logistics – and three others, were lost with him.

The tragedy did little to dim the appeal of the rally. The following year, Peugeot, then dominating world rallying, took their iconic

205 Turbo 16 on to the Dakar and won it with 1981 world champion Ari Vatanen.

Thus began an era when the world's leading rally teams took over the event. Vatanen's victory was the first of four in a row for Peugeot, two more for him, and one for fellow Finn Juha Kankkunen, another rallying great, who was eventually to become a four-time world rally champion.

Peugeot morphed into sister brand Citroën which carried on the winning run. Soon the event was a target for all sorts of car makers. Mitsubishi are serial winners – including seven consecutive wins in the early 2000s. Volkswagen has had its fair share, as well as Mini and Toyota.

The Dakar has been through three main iterations. Originally, it was a three-week trek from Paris to Dakar in Senegal, with one exception in 1992 when it travelled the full length of Africa and finished in Cape Town.

That route came to an end when the race was cancelled in 2008 after four French tourists were killed in Mauritania in December 2007, the attack blamed on a group linked to Al-Qaida. The event moved to South America in 2009, mainly to Argentina and Chile but sometimes also including Bolivia, Peru and Paraguay. And since 2020, when the pandemic forced a rethink, it has found a new home in Saudi Arabia.

Each iteration has had unique characteristics – it's current format is two weeks long when it used to be three, for instance. But all have shared the same principle – a race across a desert, with no reconnaissance allowed, competitors sleeping in makeshift camps, facing some of the toughest demands in any sport anywhere in the world.

The locations provide some of the most stunning images possible – grand desert vistas, vehicles lost in impossible expanses of aching,

shimmering beauty, the starkness and unyielding nature of the challenge reflected by the majesty and drama of the setting.

The big names keep coming, too. Recently including Fernando Alonso, one of the greatest Formula 1 drivers in history, who raced the Dakar Rally in 2020, and says he may well go back once his F1 career is finally over.

Alonso was mentored that year by his friend Carlos Sainz (Senior), who has been competing on the Dakar for nearly 20 years. Sainz, father of the F1 driver, is one of world rallying's greatest figures, becoming an icon through his battles with the likes of Colin McRae, Juha Kankkunen, Marcus Grönholm, Tommi Mäkinen, Miki Biasion and Richard Burns.

In addition to his 26 world rally wins – fourth most successful in the all-time list – Sainz has won the Dakar four times and is one of the few to experience all three versions of the event. Now in his 60s, he keeps going back: "Probably I am a little bit stupid," he jokes, but he remains a competitive force. Who could expect anything less of a man whose remorselessness, determination and strength of character earned him the nickname 'The Matador' in his heyday?

"The Dakar has changed its location," Sainz says, "but the most important thing is that when you look at the amount of retirements – which is a kind of thermometer to know whether the character has stayed – the DNA of the rally hasn't changed.

"The big challenge of the Dakar is that it is a two-week race. People need to understand that you drive blind. You have a road book, but the road book many, many times is useless. You need to drive with your eyes. You haven't gone through before, so you need to rely on what you see. And then judge your speed.

"This throws you on many occasions to misjudge many situations. Depending on the risk you want to take, there can be a lot of rewards because you are driving blind. But at the same time the rally will catch you out sooner or later if you continue to take a lot of risk.

"The characteristic is try to put the machine and the crews and the teams up to the limit, physically and mentally, and this is what makes the rally a bit special. It is very challenging. Either you like it or you hate it."

For Sainz, the African countries were the toughest, with the Sahel in Mauritania being "probably the most challenging" location. "There were days when I did 650–700km. The speeds were high. South America was a little different because the population was higher. Sometimes the heat

was terrible, sometimes it went up to 40–45°C because it was summer there, and the percentage of retirements was sometimes even higher, but it is not the same being in Argentina as in Mauritania."

For some, part of the appeal is admiring the visual splendour from afar – though the drivers rarely get a chance to appreciate it.

"Sometimes when you see the filming, you are like, 'Wow, that was a great place,'" Sainz says. "But you are so much concentrating on the driving and looking 50–100m in front of you trying to read the terrain.

"Sometimes it is more open desert and you can look at the immensity of the desert and the sea of

ABOVE: Sébastien Loeb passes some typically dramatic Arabian desert scenery on the 2024 event.

OPPOSITE TOP: Kazakhstani driver Artur Ardavichus in the Astana-sponsored MAN truck was one of forty-five to finish in that category in 2017, despite testing the limits of his suspension.

OPPOSITE BOTTOM: It's not all deserts – American driver Robby Gordon in the Mini 4 heads into the mountains on the stage from Salta, Argentina, to Uyuni, Bolivia, in 2014.

dunes you are crossing. But most of the time, you really need to be very concentrated on driving."

It's the intensity and duration of the challenge that makes the Dakar what it is. "The accident is waiting for you very, very often," Sainz says. "And the speed is quite high. With the dunes, for example, you need to always expect the worst. You brake, you go through, you brake, you go through."

"You can't see? You need to brake. Now, it's a crest or whatever. Many times you brake for not much, sometimes for nothing, and you have the feeling you are losing time. But you cannot lose this discipline, because as soon as you lose this discipline to brake in the places you need to brake, the accident is waiting for you, for sure.

"The reward of taking risks is you can gain a lot of time but you cannot do it forever."

ABOVE: Cars and bikes set off one by one on the Daka, but sometimes they concertina together, as pictured here in the dunes in 2024.

OPPOSITE TOP: By Stage 11 on January 18th, 2024, Carlos Sainz was leading the rally by a large margin and caution was the order of the day.

OPPOSITE BOTTOM LEFT: The advance of cars such as Sainz's Audi RS Q e-tron allow organisers to choose routes that the 1980s cars, such as the Peugeot 205 or Porsche 959 could never have attempted.

OPPOSITE BOTTOM RIGHT: Carlos Sainz celebrated his fourth Dakar win in 2024. The prodigious Stéphane Peterhansel is the record holder with 10 victories.

Daytona Speedway

Daytona Beach, USA

The Daytona International Speedway is the home of the most prestigious race in the most popular motorsport series in America, NASCAR (The National Association for Stock Car Auto Racing), as well as the second biggest endurance sportscar race in the world.

NASCAR, a stock car series predominantly based in America's south, stages the Daytona 500 on a 4.02km (2.50 mile) tri-oval with two of the corners banked at a precipitous 31 degrees. The steep banking guarantees a particular kind of racing known as 'drafting', where long lines of cars packed closely together slipstream each other.

The Daytona 24 Hours sportscar event is held on a 5.74km (3.56 mile) road course that incorporates the final corner of the oval and much of the first corner and winds around the infield for the rest of the lap. The Speedway circuit was the brainchild of NASCAR founder William France Sr, who wanted it to promote his fledgling series, which was founded in 1948 out of its origins in bootlegging during Prohibition, and which at the time was racing on a road course at Daytona Beach.

It was France's idea to have the banking as high as possible, to give spectators the best possible view of the track – the massive grandstand looping around the start-finish section holds 123,500 people, and an extra 40,000 or so can be accommodated elsewhere depending on the track layout used.

To build the banking, about 24 million cubic metres (31 million cubic yards) of soil had to be excavated from the infield. The hole that was left has become a lake, as a result of the high water table in the beachside location.

The track hosted the first race of the 1959 NASCAR season and has kept its position ever since. Its popularity can be judged by the fact that it rivals the Indianapolis 500, regarded as the biggest race in the US and one of the three most high-profile in the world for television audiences.

Daytona hosted its first sportscar race on the road course the year it opened, too. Initially, it was a three-hour event, but by 1966 had become the 24 Hours race.

In both cases, it is the history that makes the track special. Richard 'The King' Petty, the most successful NASCAR driver in history with 200 race wins, is also the record-holder at the Daytona 500, which he won seven times. Other major NASCAR names, such as Cale Yarborough, Jeff Gordon and Jimmie Johnson, are among the multiple winners.

A quirk of history is that Dale Earnhardt, arguably the leading driver for much of the 1980s and 1990s, won the 500 only once in 1998, having previously been hindered by reliability problems,

OPPOSITE: Joey Logano and Michael McDowell lead the field to start the NASCAR Daytona 500 in February 2024. The Speedway's grandstands have a permanent capacity of 101,500 with the option to increase to 125,000.

LEFT: Logano, driving the Penske-run Ford Mustang Dark Horse, leads the first of two Daytona 500 qualifying races in 2024.

crashes or other misfortunes. And yet, with 34 victories across other series at the track – including Daytona 500 qualifying races and the Pepsi 400 – he is the most successful driver in history of the Speedway.

Earnhardt's win came only three years before the track claimed his life. 'The Intimidator', as he was known because of his aggressive style, tangled with another car on the last lap of the 500, and he crashed nose first into the wall at an estimated speed of 257km/h (160mph). He died of a basilar skull fracture.

Earnhardt's death led to safety improvements, including the adoption of the Head And Neck Safety (HANS) device – which guards against such injuries by restricting the movement of the head in impacts and is now mandated across

motorsport. Impact-absorbing barriers were also introduced on high-speed ovals, where before there were only exposed concrete walls.

The 24 Hours, too, is steeped in its own history – the first edition in 1966 was also the first victory for the iconic Ford GT40, and started the famous rivalry with Ferrari, recently immortalised in Hollywood film *Ford v Ferrari* starring Matt Damon and Christian Bale. Its cachet is enhanced by the fact that winners are given a special Rolex Daytona watch.

"You can buy a Daytona," says F1 driver Kevin Magnussen, who raced in the 24 Hours in 2021 and 2022, "but not the one you win. Every race driver wants that watch. It's one of the most sought-after trophies in the world."

OPPOSITE: The cars lines up before the 24-hour race in 2019.

BELOW: Joey Logano (22) gets involved in a multi-car collision in Turn 3 during the Daytona 500 and was one of ten DNFs.

BOTTOM: A night view of the 24 Hours of Daytona from 2018, a field which included Fernando Alonso, Helio Castroneves, Bruno Senna, Felipe Nasr, Sam Bird and Alex Brundle.

Donington Park

Castle Donington, England

Donington Park has hosted only one Formula 1 race, but what a race it was. The 1993 European Grand Prix is remembered by many as arguably the greatest drive in the career of arguably the greatest F1 driver of all time.

Ayrton Senna won the race for McLaren by 1 minute and 23 seconds from the Williams of Damon Hill, with the Brazilian's arch-rival Alain Prost lapped in the other Williams.

The raw statistics are impressive enough. But it was the details of the win and the nature of Senna's superiority that really mark out the race among so many remarkable performances over his career.

In particular, Senna's first lap was enough to inspire awe in all those watching, including his rivals in the race that day. Karl Wendlinger, one of the drivers Senna passed in the course of it, said it was like he was "walking on water". Two-time world champion Emerson Fittipaldi, watching at home in Miami, described it as "pure genius".

Senna qualified fourth in the dry, unable to match the superior Williams FW15Cs of Prost and Hill and was beaten also by the Benetton of rising star Michael Schumacher. But race day was wet and cold, a typically grey, drizzly British spring day. Senna didn't get the greatest start and was passed on the run to the first corner by Wendlinger's Sauber. But what happened next was remarkable.

Schumacher, also passed by Wendlinger on the inside on the run to the first corner, forced Senna wide and although the McLaren ducked back to the inside of the Benetton, Senna entered the first corner, Redgate, in fifth place. But he exited the corner strongly and passed Schumacher as he did so.

From there, the track starts to head downhill through the Craner Curves, a challenging high-speed right-left. Senna went around the outside of Wendlinger through the left and was clear in third as he entered the Old Hairpin – a misnomer for a fast right-hander with a compression at the apex at the foot of the Craners.

Exiting here with much more speed than Hill, he tracked the second Williams through the two left-hand kinks that lead into the uphill approach to the right-hander of McLean's, where Senna pulled a straightforward outbraking manoeuvre.

Now only Prost was ahead, by a good few car lengths, but Senna closed in through Coppice, another right with an uphill entry, and then the chicane that leads into the Melbourne loop, before diving inside Prost on the downhill approach to the Melbourne hairpin, brushing off the Frenchman's defence.

This writer was at Donington Park that day, standing at the chicane for the first few laps in the chill wet fog. Almost as soon as the race started, there was a sense that something special was afoot. The circuit commentary was barely audible – as was common at grands prix

OPPOSITE: Cars line up for the start on a damp English spring afternoon that felt more like a club meeting than an international grand prix.

TOP: Senna and Prost together on the Donington podium.

ABOVE: Senna dives inside Prost under braking for the Melbourne hairpin to take the lead. Damon Hill is in car zero because Williams had not retained World Champion Nigel Mansell who had the option on race number one.

back then — but a buzz started to pass through the crowd, and there was a gasp among the spectators as the cars burst into view at the end of Starkey's Straight with Senna already on Prost's tail, and clearly about to go by.

Once into the lead, Senna was in a league of his own all afternoon. He pulled out 7 seconds on Prost in the next three laps, and spent the rest of the race underlining his superiority over not just the two Williams drivers, but the whole field.

It was a race defined by skill and confidence, and a willingness to take risks with the weather. After a few laps, the track began to dry as the drizzle eased, and Prost first pegged Senna and then began to inch back towards him. But then the rain returned — it never really stopped the whole time, just varied in intensity — and Senna stretched away again.

Senna's one stroke of luck arrived when he came in at about three-quarters distance for wets but McLaren weren't ready for him, and he had to

"Driving with slicks in damp and really slippery conditions was tremendous effort. You just don't get the feeling from the car and you just have to commit yourself to certain corners, and you just can be off."

Senna was presented with his trophy by circuit owner Tom Wheatcroft, who had finally achieved a long-time dream to host F1 at the track he bought in 1971. A local businessman, Wheatcroft had a collection of classic racing cars, which he housed in a museum at the track. Until it closed in 2018, it was the largest collection of grand prix cars in the world.

Before and after the 1993 race, Donington was a track that hosted lesser categories. Its history is significant. It was the first permanent parkland circuit in the country, and ended the monopoly Brooklands had as a British race track. The roads of the Donington Hall Estate were first used for racing in 1931, when local garage owner Fred Craner, a motorcycle racer in his spare time, approached estate owner John Gillies, for permission to use them.

In 1933, Craner, after whom the curves were named, won permission to build a permanent track, and by 1935 the first Donington Park Grand Prix was held.

The final two events before World War II in 1937 and 1938 attracted the state-sponsored Mercedes and Auto Union teams that were dominating grand prix racing at the time. The thundering silver machines, years ahead in technology compared to their contemporary rivals, made quite a stir. The races were won by Bernd Rosemeyer and Tazio Nuvolari, two of the greatest drivers of the inter-war period.

The track was requisitioned as a military vehicle depot in the war and racing only returned to Donington Park when Wheatcroft took it over. Two years before his death in 2009, Wheatcroft

continue through the pits. Ironically, as the pit lane was a short cut, he set the fastest lap.

He stayed out until the rain really began to increase in intensity with about 10 laps to go, coming in for a fourth time to fit the wets that took him to the end of the race. Prost, meanwhile, made seven stops, always seeming to make the wrong call on tyres.

Senna said afterwards: "I am speechless, really over the moon. Conditions like this is gambling, and it's taking chances that pays off. We gambled good and we got the result.

"At the start I decided to really go for it, before the Williams had the time to settle down. They do have technical superiority and we felt this was the best tactic. And then so many things happened that I find it hard to remember.

sold the lease of the track to a local company, which contrived a deal to take over the British Grand Prix from Silverstone from 2010. But the company failed to raise the necessary funds and the deal collapsed, leaving a half-altered circuit in disarray.

Ownership returned to the Wheatcroft family for a while but nowadays the Donington Park racing business is owned by the Motor Sport Vision company of former F1 driver Jonathan Palmer, which also runs Brands Hatch, Cadwell Park, Oulton Park and Snetterton, and dominates the UK national racing scene outside Silverstone. Palmer has a lease on the Donington Park estate until 2038.

OPPOSITE TOP: Tazio Nuvolari driving for Auto Union at the 1938 Donington Grand Prix. The original picture caption read: 'The Italian master was in superb form and led most of the race, except when forced to his pit for a plug change which only seemed to make him try harder. It was a very popular victory.'

OPPOSITE BOTTOM: Donington has long been the backdrop for epic tussles in the British Touring Car Championship.

ABOVE: Cars stream through the Craner Curves, named after Fred Craner, the man who made it all possible.

Fuji Speedway

Oyama, Japan

Fuji Speedway is one of Japan's two most famous race circuits. But despite having the advantage of an enviable backdrop in the shape of the perfect cone of its namesake volcano, Mount Fuji, it is in the perpetual shadow of the nation's other track – Suzuka (see page 194).

That is despite the fact that Fuji was the first Japanese circuit to host Formula 1, that three of the four grands prix it has held are stone-cold classics, and all four notable in their own way. Fuji's downfall is that its majesty comes from its setting, while Suzuka's is from its challenge.

In truth, almost any circuit in the world pales in comparison to Suzuka, and Fuji's 4.56km (2.83 miles) are no match for Suzuka's 5.81km (3.60 miles), featuring only one really interesting corner – the long right-hander of 100R. On a clear day, having Mount Fuji right next door cannot be beaten as a setting, and the long pit straight provides good overtaking. All too often, though, the venue is marked by low clouds and damp weather and no sighting of Fujiyama.

Such was the case at the circuit's most celebrated race, the 1976 Japanese Grand Prix, the race that decided the title battle between McLaren's James Hunt and Ferrari's Niki Lauda.

Held in atrocious wet weather, Lauda, still recovering from his near-fatal accident at the Nürburgring a couple of months before, withdrew after two laps, declaring the conditions

ABOVE: James Hunt followed by McLaren teammate Jochen Mass in the race that determined the 1976 World Championship at the Fuji Speedway.

OPPOSITE: The No.50 Ferrari 499P of Fuoco, Molina and Nielsen in action during the 6 Hours of Fuji race in 2023.

unsafe. The race continued, though, and after a somewhat hectic afternoon that included a pit stop to replace a punctured tyre, Hunt finished third, enough to clinch the title by one point.

Fuji hosted another grand prix a year later, but two spectators standing in a restricted area were killed when they were hit by Gilles Villeneuve's Ferrari, which had been involved in a collision with Ronnie Peterson's six-wheel Tyrrell P34.

When Japan returned to the F1 calendar 10 years on, it was at Suzuka, and it was a case of instant love. Fuji was taken over by Toyota in 2000, and the car manufacturer decided after entering F1 in 2002 that it wanted to compete with its rival Honda for its home race, and it struck a deal to take over the event in 2007.

Just as in 1976, this race was held in heavy rain, and was notable for a dominant performance from Lewis Hamilton, which appeared to put him on the cusp of a debut season world title,

especially as McLaren teammate Fernando Alonso, his car damaged after a collision with Sebastian Vettel's Toro Rosso, crashed trying to keep up.

Vettel had a torrid afternoon – he was also responsible for taking out Mark Webber's Red Bull when he collided with the Australian – and almost Hamilton, too, behind a safety car.

A year later, the 2008 event saw title rivals Hamilton and Felipe Massa eliminated early on, and turned into one of Alonso's greatest ever victories. Back at Renault after his fall-out with McLaren, the Spaniard took control of strategy from the cockpit and put in a mesmeric middle stint of consistency and searing pace to beat Robert Kubica's BMW.

That was the final Japanese Grand Prix at Fuji. The 2007 race had featured complaints from spectators, and when there were poor ticket sales for the follow-up event in 2008, it was

decided to alternate the race with Suzuka. When Toyota withdrew from F1 in 2009 following the global financial crash, Suzuka was left on its own, to no-one's regret. Fuji's big international event since then has been its annual round of the World Endurance Championship. But it remains integral to motorsport in the country, hosting Formula Nippon, the top national single-seater category, touring cars, GTs and many other events.

Goodwood

Chichester, England

For a long time, Goodwood circuit in West Sussex was most famous as the place where two illustrious careers came to an end.

In the spring of 1962, Stirling Moss crashed his Lotus there in the high-speed St Mary's corner and it was serious enough that he never raced at the highest level again. Moss realised when he tried a return more than a year later that his concentration had gone and that he "could kill myself quite easily".

Eight years later, in June 1970, Bruce McLaren, a leading driver of the 1960s and founder of the company that bears his name, was killed testing a McLaren M8D sportscar destined for the North American Can-Am endurance racing series. The rear bodywork failed and the car spun and hit a trackside marshals' post. There were no safety facilities at Goodwood.

That fact had already sounded the death knell for the track as a venue for major races in 1966, when the circuit owners declined to modify it for safety reasons. Prior to that, the 3.86km (2.40 mile) track had vied with Silverstone for the status of the UK's leading motorsport venue.

Since 1998, though, Goodwood has undergone a revival – literally, for that is the name of an annual race meeting held on the old track, unchanged, to celebrate classic cars from the race track's operating era – 1948–1966. Goodwood Revival joined the Festival of Speed, which was inaugurated in 1993, and involves notable cars giving demonstration runs up the drive to Goodwood House and beyond. The events have been a huge success, with crowds of more than 100,000 attending each day.

Both events are the brainchild of the owner of the estate, the 11th Duke of Richmond, Charles Gordon-Lennox (previously the Earl of March), and both involve an element of risk. There are still no gravel traps or safety barriers on the Goodwood circuit – only grass and banks, just like in the old days. And the drive at the Festival of Speed is flanked by thousands of people as cars blast by at significant speeds.

Racing driver and TV presenter Karun Chandhok, who races and works at both events, says: "Charles March has heavily leant on that whole ethos of motorsport at Goodwood being that nod to the past, so he gets the buy-in of everybody.

"Nobody goes there and complains that the circuit is too dangerous; we all go there with the attitude that you can leave some margin and it's one of those circuits where you appreciate what people had to go through when racing in the 1950s and 1960s.

"It feels old-school. There are lots of camber changes and bumps, and the way the edge of the track is with the drop on to the grass is how you imagine circuits used to be probably going back to the 1980s or even early 1990s. Let alone going back to the 1950s."

Chandhok, though, vocalises a thought that occurs to many who see these old cars being driven relatively hard on a track that, even back in the mid-1960s, was considered too dangerous.

"Every year we think: 'There is going to be a big one there one day.' And I pray that there isn't but, in reality, you are playing the odds, because the cars and drivers are getting more and more competitive and brave and aggressive.

"You do think in some ways there are things that need to be done at the Festival of Speed as well: 100,000 people standing beside the driveway and those cars are going bloody fast.

"But Goodwood in general, and Charles March in particular, thrive on that brand: 'We are different and we are an event that is going to be against the grain of this modern world of big Tarmac run-offs and health and safety.' They are the antithesis of that."

INDY 500	
1	●●●
1	10
2	21
3	6
4	14
5	5
6	9
7	7
8	11
9	66
10	8
11	55
12	12
13	33
14	3
15	27
16	20
17	2
18	23
19	28
20	06
21	26
22	60
23	18
24	98
25	29
26	78
27	77
28	50
29	44
30	45
31	51
32	30
33	24

Indianapolis Motor Speedway

Indianapolis, Indiana, USA

America is famed for its banked oval tracks, and the Indianapolis Motor Speedway (IMS) is the most famous of all. It's ironic, then, that the home of the iconic Indy 500 is not really a traditional oval at all.

Ovals are typically two straights joined by two corners, in the shape of, yes, an oval. Sometimes the straights are both exactly that; sometimes one of them is curved to form a third 'corner' that isn't really anything of the sort.

Indianapolis is different. It is, as 2003 winner Gil de Ferran told me for this book before his untimely death at the age of just 56 in 2023, "like a big, old road course".

This sounds counter-intuitive for a track that does share many of the characteristics of an oval – there are only left-handed corners, and it is very, very fast. De Ferran explained: "It's got four 90-degree corners and they're all a little bit different in character even though they are designed to be exactly the same.

"They all have slightly different undulations, the wind hits them a little bit differently, so they hardly ever feel the same. And unlike, shall we say, a more traditional oval, you have very little line choice. You do have some but not as much as you do in let's call it a more traditional high-banked oval."

All of this partly explains the almost overpowering mystique of Indianapolis. It's a track and an event like nothing else. By far America's most important motor race, the Indy 500 holds an imposing position in global motorsport as one of the three 'biggest races in the world', along with the Monaco Grand Prix and Le Mans 24 Hours (see pages 72 and 12).

Indianapolis is the third oldest permanent race track in the world after the Milwaukee Mile (see page 152) and Brooklands, and the first to be called a Speedway.

OPPOSITE: Dominated by the IMS's distinctive pagoda, the Indy 500 gets underway in 2023. In May, naturally.

BELOW: Gil de Ferran won the 1992 British F3 championship, finished third in F3000 in 1994, but then switched to IndyCar in 1995 and never looked back. This Team Penske photo is from 2003, when he won the Indy 500.

Its seating capacity of nearly 260,000 makes it the world's largest-capacity sports stadium. Races tend to be slow-burn events punctuated by terrifying high-speed crashes, building always to a dramatic climax, usually involving slipstreaming.

Indianapolis held its first race in 1909, the layout exactly the same as it is today, a 4km (2.5 mile) Speedway with four shallow-banked 90-degree corners. Since then, in terms of the racing circuit, only the track surface has changed. Soil and loose stones for the first race, it was switched almost immediately to brick, at a time when only a few miles of public roads were paved.

This surface earned the track a nickname that has endured to this day: The Brickyard. Although the turns were all converted to asphalt by 1937, and the whole track in 1961, a tiny section of the original bricks remains in a strip three feet wide at the start-finish line.

Indy has been the heart and soul of American motor racing ever since it was built. The so-called 'Golden Age' of the 1910s and 1920s earned the 500 a global standing. It survived the Great Depression of the 1930s with the 'Junkyard' formula, when the rules were simplified to make it easier and cheaper for people to enter.

The 1950s brought the roadster era, and by then the race's international status was so great that it was made a round of the nascent Formula 1 world championship for 10 years, even though none of the Indy drivers raced in F1 during that time, and only Ferrari's Alberto Ascari competed at Indy, in 1952.

In the 1960s, although no longer part of the F1 championship, European teams and drivers began to enter the 500, and exported the rear-engined revolution they had pioneered 'across the pond'.

AJ Foyt, one of the race's leading figures, took the last front-engined win in 1964 – four years after Ferrari did the same in F1 at Monza. It was fitting that Jim Clark, the greatest driver of his era, sealed the first rear-engined Indy win when he made a second entry in the race with the Lotus team in 1965 – the year he won his second Formula 1 title. Another F1 world champion, Graham Hill, won the next one on his debut the following year.

Clark and Hill fought out the victory between them in 1966, in a race that burnished Clark's legend despite Hill being declared the victor. Clark's Lotus had handling problems and he spun twice during the race, each time somehow without hitting the wall. Clark's skills in saving himself from disaster stunned the US regulars. One of the times, he came off Turn Four with the engine stalled and the car going backwards. Clark cooly flicked it around, selected a gear and popped the clutch to get going again.

The finish between the two drivers was disputed. Clark and Hill both drove to Victory Lane, and Hill was awarded victory. Some believe that Clark had actually won, despite his problems, and that the scorers had mistakenly given one of his laps to teammate Al Unser.

This era marked the advent of some of American racing's biggest ever stars. Foyt had a strong rivalry with Mario Andretti, who started racing in the late 1950s, won the Indy 500 in 1969, the 1978 world title during a 14-year F1 career, and

OPPOSITE: An aerial view of 'The Brickyard'. The infield course was created to provide a suitable alternative for Formula 1 cars, and has subsequently been used for other series.

TOP RIGHT: Jim Clark is interviewed in 1965 after becoming the first Brit to win the Indy 500 and the simply enormous Borg-Warner trophy behind him.

RIGHT: Clark's Ford-powered Lotus 38 was the first rear-engined car to win America's blue riband race in 1964.

raced IndyCars until 1994, becoming the oldest ever winner at 53 years old.

Brothers Bobby and Al Unser also emerged at this time. Foyt and Al Unser set the all-time record of winning the 500 four times, since equalled only by 1980s star Rick Mears, and Brazilian Hélio Castroneves, who was De Ferran's teammate at Penske for a while.

The power of the Indy 500 and its unchallenged status in American racing was demonstrated in the 1990s when Speedway owner Tony George fell out with the organisers of the CART Championship, as IndyCar racing was known at the time, and formed a breakaway series called the Indy Racing League (IRL). At the time, CART was at its absolute zenith, with European-raised stars such as De Ferran, Alex Zanardi, Juan

Pablo Montoya and Dario Franchitti joining the American regulars in cars that even to this day look like the aesthetic ideal of a muscular single-seater racer. Nigel Mansell paved the way for this influx with his move from F1 to CART/IndyCar in

BELOW: Indy rookie Nigel Mansell pits for the first time during his debut Indianapolis appearance in 1993, driving for the Newman/Haas team.

1993, when he became the only man ever to win back-to-back F1 and IndyCar titles.

Even so, the power of Indianapolis eventually killed CART. The two championships tried to go it alone for a while, but the gravity of the Indy 500 made it impossible. Although CART was the stronger championship, its teams and drivers could not afford to miss Indy – commercial imperatives demanded their presence. And in 2002 US motorsport titan Roger Penske, who had been loyal to CART from 1996, made the decision to move his team over to the IRL. Ganassi, another major team, followed him a year later. CART's time was over and the two series unified.

As a driver, De Ferran was one of the biggest of the big names at the heart of this period. He won the CART title for Penske in both 2001 and 2002, when he was also third in the IRL. And in 2003, after suffering a broken back in a massive crash

at the Phoenix oval early in the year, he returned for the Indy 500 and won the race. De Ferran raced in Europe before moving to America and remains the holder of the world closed-course speed record, with a 388.541km/h (241.428mph) lap at the California Speedway at Fontana in 2000. Eloquent and intelligent, no-one has been better able to describe the unique difficulty of driving at Indianapolis since.

The track looks straightforward – it is, after all, 'just' a huge rectangle – but it is actually one of the most demanding tracks around. De Ferran said qualifying at Indy was, "probably the most challenging thing I've done in a racing car". The trick for one four-lap, 16km (10 mile) qualifying run at Indy is to take the track flat-out all the way around, while running as little downforce as possible. The cars are trimmed out so much in the quest for the highest average speed that it becomes, in De Ferran's words, "like driving on ice at 230mph (370km/h)".

ABOVE LEFT: Formula 1's arrival at Indianapolis involved the cars running in the reverse direction on part of the oval, but fans' loyalty was tested to the limit when runners using Michelin tyres failed to take the grid in 2005 and the race was run with six cars.

TOP: Fernando Alonso's Renault crosses 'The Brickyard'.

ABOVE: Michael Schumacher took the F1 race victory in 2004.

"You're so short on grip," he said. "And if you start lifting, then the attitude of the car starts changing, the ride height starts changing and it gets even worse. It's a knife-edge situation, and the other interesting thing is a lot of the time you just have to commit and then once you're

in the corner you kind of figure out what the hell's going on. Because if you are conservative, you have already lost the time.

"And if you get into trouble in Indy, it is very difficult to get out of trouble. In other ovals sometimes, you back off, you run a little wider, hopefully you don't get into the grey (part of the track, where tyre debris and dirt reduces grip). You have a little bit more room to manoeuvre. In Indy, you commit to go flat. You start to get into trouble, and it's like, 'Holy shit. Now what?'"

One of the myriad things that can get drivers into trouble at Indianapolis is windspeed and its direction. As a massive, open layout in the middle of a sparse, open, flat landscape in the US Mid West, the Speedway is particularly exposed.

Driving into the wind gives a car more grip, especially at the front. A tail wind gives less grip, but also oversteer – a loose rear end, the last thing you want when you're cornering at 370km/h (230mph) and margins are tiny, and any error can put you in the wall. If the wind is coming from the side, a driver turns in with oversteer, and comes out of the corner with understeer. This, De Ferran said with withering understatement, is "not a lot of fun".

"So that's why one of the first things you do is look at where the wind is," he said. "That information is crucial for the driver. Because you can make a few adjustments, you can turn in a little bit earlier or later, choose slightly different things. There is a wind sock on top of the pagoda on the start-finish straight, and the teams normally have wind data from around the track. But the wind is crucial because if you're doing a new-tyre run in qualifying trim, you have to commit, so you're deciding ahead of time what you're going to do, so you need to have the maximum amount of information to be able to make good decisions."

De Ferran told an anecdote that sums up what the drivers are often facing, and which competitive pride means they rarely discuss. He said the most impressive thing he ever saw in nearly 30 years of attending the Indy 500 as a driver or senior team figure was Hélio Castroneves's pole run when they were Penske teammates in 2003.

ABOVE LEFT: Gil de Ferran with Fernando Alonso after the Spaniard clocked the seventh fastest time in qualifying for the Indy 500 in 2017.

ABOVE: De Ferran advised Alonso at his first attempt at Indy with McLaren Honda and Andretti in 2017. He ran competitively, but suffered an engine failure in the closing stages.

"It was the year I won the race but I was coming back from my huge accident at Phoenix," De Ferran said. "Hélio started the month with a bang. He was fast every day, his car was good, he was comfortable, everything was fine. My month was very gradual. I had missed a race with my injuries, and I went from the first day back in the car thinking '****ing hell, I'm going to have to retire here', to actually trading fastest times with Scott Dixon and Hélio on what they call 'fast Friday', the day before qualifying – I was very confident.

"I was like: 'Okay, I'm good here.' I knew I was in good shape. But... 'Fast Friday' was 70°F (21°C), no wind, literally perfect conditions. And we kept trimming the car out more and more and more. Very little wing in the car.

"Wake up Saturday morning. Man, it was 50°F (10°C), the wind was blowing a steady 25mph (40km/h) with gusts of 40mph (64km/h). I went out to warm up and I am literally full opposite lock in Turn Two, trying to open on the second corner of the lap. And I'm thinking: '**** me.' God knows how I didn't crash.

"And so I came into the pits, and I was like, '****ing hell, man, this is hard.' So we put a little bit more understeer in the car and went out again. Another massive moment. I was like 'Oh, my God, this is terrible.'

"So we go back to the garage, trying to decide what to do. Hélio's back in and he's also white. He's like, 'What the hell's going on, man?' And I'm like, 'I don't know! That really nice car we had yesterday has literally gone.'

ABOVE: Roger Penske stands on the pitwall as his team work on the set-up for the qualifying week.

RIGHT: Gil De Ferran and teammate Hélio Castroneves climb the fencing after Gil's 2003 Indy 500 victory.

BELOW RIGHT: De Ferran celebrating his Indy victory with his wife Angela and his son Luke and daughter Anna. Gil was behind the wheel, racing with his son at the Concourse Club in Florida in 2023 when he suffered what would be a fatal heart attack.

"So we are both struggling throughout the day. And essentially after three or four tries of scaring myself to death, right, I gave up. I said, 'I will just put another degree or two of rear wing and just go out and qualify because I can't do this any more.' So I did that and did a reasonable time, qualified 10th or whatever it was.

"Hélio, on the other hand, he kept insisting. Kept trying, kept trying and he did a qualifying run at the end of the day that was the fastest lap of the month. And, honestly, I saw the data, he was perfect. Literally perfect. And I'm like: 'You know what, dude. My hat's off to you.'"

Las Vegas Strip Circuit

Nevada, USA

Las Vegas is all about the money. It's about the casino hotels making it and their guests losing it in return for being entertained – and the Formula 1 grand prix in the Nevada city lays this relationship bare.

The race, first held in 2023 (the 1980s version was the Caesars Palace Grand Prix), is the sport's new poster event, created by owners Liberty Media to grow Formula 1's profile in the States, where Las Vegas has been added to the US Grand Prix in Austin, Texas, and the Miami Grand Prix in Florida.

Liberty succeeded in organising a race that incorporates the famous Las Vegas Strip where previous commercial chief Bernie Ecclestone failed because, this time, the casinos bought into it. The hotels could see from the investment Liberty Media was putting in that they could make money from the race.

While each of the US races has its own distinct character, there are no prizes for guessing which is most important to Liberty – the US giant invested upwards of $500m in buying land in the heart of Las Vegas, on which it built a pit complex. And it provided a metaphor for the extent to which money trumps all in Vegas.

At the inaugural event there was not even room for a media centre, with Formula 1 management preferring to maximise its income by devoting as much space as possible to hospitality. The media was housed in a hotel a ten-minute walk away.

Those corporate entertainment packages did not come cheap – $50,000 was the price of one offered by the Wynn Hotel in the Paddock Club above the pits. Compared to that, the $11,247 per person for three days at the Bellagio Hotel's Fountain Club – on a platform that had a view to die for, with the cars blasting down the famous Strip on one side, and the lights, water and music show of the hotel's famous fountains on the other – looked good value.

The world champion, Red Bull's Max Verstappen, went into the weekend expressing his distaste for the race, saying it was "99% show and 1% sporting event". His remarks did not go down well with F1, not least because they bore an essential, if inconvenient, truth.

OPPOSITE: Max Verstappen's Red Bull approaches the Sphere on his way to another victory in 2023... although the only one dressed as Elvis.

LEFT: Nelson Piquet (5) in the Brabham-Ford on his way to winning the 1981 World Championship in the Caesars Palace parking lot.

This race certainly raised the question of the balance of competition and entertainment with which so many sports are wrestling in the twenty-first century. Here, it was mainly about the show.

Verstappen was not the only person to find it all a bit distasteful. For all that, though, the Las Vegas Grand Prix worked – as sport, entertainment and business. MGM Resorts, the owner of the Bellagio and other major hotels, said the grand prix was the highest grossing event in the company's history – and on what is traditionally the slowest weekend of the year in Las Vegas, the one before Thanksgiving.

On track, Red Bull drivers Max Verstappen and Sergio Perez, and Ferrari's Charles Leclerc staged arguably the best race of the season on the 6.20km (3.85 mile), 17-corner circuit marked out through the heart of the city, passing some of its most famous landmarks. This included the giant Sphere, where the grand prix was considered so important that rock band U2 had to pause their residency there for the race.

There were complaints about the timetable too; Daniel Ricciardo spoke for everyone when he said a weekend on which practice and qualifying both finished in the early hours of the morning, and the race started at 10pm had left everyone in the sport – drivers, team personnel and media – "a little bit delirious and a little bit hallucinatory".

But Mercedes F1 boss Toto Wolff summed up the general optimism about the future of Formula 1 and Las Vegas among the sport's chiefs when he said: "Spectacular race, great audiences, mega event."

ABOVE: Max takes the plaudits (and his straight-talking) from dad Jos alongside manager Raymond Vermeulen.

TOP: Vegas branding was everywhere – even the kerbing.

OPPOSITE: It was clear to see that F1 commercial rights holder Liberty Media had staked a massive investment in race facilities.

Laguna Seca

Monterey, USA

It says a lot for the status of Laguna Seca in California that when Liberty Media was scouting for new grand prix venues in the United States after taking over Formula 1, it was one of the first places they considered.

In the end, a deal was not possible. Laguna's owners would not remove the track's most famous corner, the Corkscrew, and F1 was not prepared to race there with it, because the lack of run-off area did not meet safety standards, and the topography meant nothing could be done about that.

F1 has moved on now, with new races in Miami and Las Vegas, which is in many ways a shame, because Laguna would make a great venue for a grand prix.

Inaugurated in 1957, Laguna is situated on the Monterey peninsula, near the coastal towns of Carmel-by-the Sea and Monterey, two of the loveliest places in America. Its name means 'dry lagoon' in Spanish – the area was once a lake. The track perches on a hillside of central Californian coastal scrub and is only 3.56km (2.23 miles) long. But it packs a lot into that short distance.

The start-finish straight plunges downhill, into a long, double-apex hairpin, now named after American motorsport legend and 1978 F1 world champion Mario Andretti, who took his final IndyCar victory at Laguna in 1994 at the age of 54.

McLaren Racing chief executive Zak Brown, a former racing driver who attends the Monterey

historic car festival every year and drives Laguna in his collection of classic racing cars, says the run up through the kink of Turn 6, the Corkscrew and then two banked corners as the track plunges back down the hill towards its finish, "is about a cool a sequence as anywhere in the world".

It's easy to see why the Corkscrew is so famous. It looks incredibly spectacular – cars reach the top of a hill, and then take a precipitous plunge as they turn to the left and then immediately right, dropping rapidly downwards.

The corner's fame was heightened by Alex Zanardi, who made a spectacular pass on Bryan Herta to win the IndyCar finale in 1996 – a pass

that in F1 would definitely have been ruled illegal for exceeding track limits on the second part of the chicane, but which in the more relaxed world of US racing was deemed fair enough.

But for all its visual drama, the Corkscrew's reputation is in some ways overblown, at least as a driving challenge.

"It's not an unbelievable driving corner," Brown says, and Gil de Ferran, who won his maiden

OPPOSITE: Cars take to the Corkscrew in the 2019 8-hour GT race, part of the Intercontinental GT Challenge Series.

BELOW: Alex Zanardi (4) of Italy passes and holds off Bryan Herta to win the Bank of America 300 at the Monterey Grand Prix in 1996, clinching the IndyCar title.

IndyCar race at Laguna in 1995, agreed. "You can't see the apex, so you just go, 'Okay, turn,' and then as soon as you hit the first apex, you turn to the other side and mash the gas."

Both agree, though, that the next two corners are special. "That left-right sequence after Corkscrew is awesome," Brown says, "because they're both banked and they're fast."

"I love that corner (after the Corkscrew)," said De Ferran, who raced both IndyCars and sportscars at Laguna. "You're coming out of the Corkscrew sort of short-shifting because the car is struggling for traction there a lot. You short-shift all the way to fourth and then you go in full speed. In the sportscar it was flat. The car does a compression event there. The car starts hitting the ground, it's quite a challenging corner.

"And the next one is the same, you go in and then there's a huge banking increase there, which makes it quite interesting. It requires a lot of technique on how you approach these corners that have quite a lot of change in banking from entry to middle to exit."

In fact, De Ferran believed there were no boring corners at Laguna. "Because of all the elevation changes and the challenges of where the corner is banked, where it's not, where the car loses load. As a driver, there is a lot to exploit and explore."

Laguna hosted an IndyCar race from 1983 until 2004, when it was shifted to Sonoma Raceway in the wine country north of San Francisco. It finally returned to what many people consider its rightful place as the climax of the IndyCar season in 2018.

For Brown, there are plenty of reasons to love Laguna. "It's also one of the best spectator tracks," he says, "because you can walk the whole perimeter. At Turn 6, the cars are kind of coming underneath you. The track is awesome. It always was a huge finale race."

TOP: Laguna Seca has been the host of Rolex Monterey Historic Automobile Races. In 2006 there was a fine assembly of classic Cooper racing machinery.

ABOVE: Scott McLaughlin (3) challenges Felix Rosenqvist (6) for the lead coming into the Andretti hairpin during the 2023 Firestone Grand Prix. Romain Grosjean is mid-pack.

OPPOSITE: An aerial view of Laguna Seca with the Corkscrew far left. Cars run anti-clockwise.

London ExCel

London, England

The Formula E track in the docklands area of East London is the world's only motorsport venue that is both indoors and outdoors.

The 2.09km (1.30 mile) track starts inside the ExCel Arena, descends a ramp to leave the building and then after tracking west to east on a perimeter road, goes back up a second ramp and returns inside.

For Sam Bird, one of the all-electric championship's most experienced drivers, this track is, "not necessarily the most exciting in terms of overtaking but it's super-interesting with regards to the layout. What they have been able to create is quite cool for the spectators, especially indoors."

For Bird, the uniqueness of the track is in the disparity between the surface inside the building and outside – and the transition between them.

"The grip level on the inside is the highest of the season and the grip outside is one of the lowest," Bird says. On top of this, where the asphalt changes from one to another, there also happen to be metal strips about 30cm (12in) wide which are the guiding slats for the ExCel's large sliding doors.

"When we transition," Bird says, "we have to take this into account with our steering angles, our speed through the corner and our turn-in point and it makes it really interesting."

On the way out of the arena at Turn Four, drivers have to go into the corner slower than expected, because they are going to lose grip through the second half of the bend. And on the way back in,

at Turn 19, they can carry in much more speed than would be appropriate for the initial level of grip because the corner will grip up halfway through.

There are other challenges, too. Not only are the grip levels very different inside and out, but the asphalt is "super-smooth" inside the building but "very, very bumpy" outside. This means a compromised set-up, Bird says. "If we were running all indoors, it's flat as a pancake and we'd be running the car on the deck, but we have the outdoor bit, so we have to run the car kind of in the sky."

The ramp that leads back into the building for the final two corners causes yet another problem.

"If you were to stay flat out at the top of the ramp," Bird says, "you are firstly going to miss your braking point and secondly you will potentially go over power because you will be airborne and then have to brake." In Formula E, going over the permitted maximum power output (350kw in qualifying and in 'attack mode', 300kw for 'normal' racing) results in a penalty.

All in all, it's quite the tricky little track.

Formula E is not to everyone's tastes and it continues to struggle for audiences a decade after its inception. But for Bird it has earned its place on the motorsport smörgåsbord. "We are there to entertain people," he says, "and they do get value for money with regard to overtaking, thrills, spills, crashes, dramas. They do get that. It's not the pinnacle, but it is dramatic."

TOP: The unique start-finish straight at ExCel is located indoors along with the pit lane and the teams' pit facilities.

ABOVE: Jake Dennis on his way to the 2023 Formula E world title at his home race. In 2014 Dennis was sharing podiums in European F3 with Esteban Ocon and Max Verstappen.

OPPOSITE: London's ePrix started life on a Battersea Park 'street' circuit but has found a permanent home at the ExCel.

Long Beach

California, USA

John Watson won five grands prix in a Formula 1 career that stretched from 1973 to the early 1980s, and he saved the best for last. The Northern Irishman's victory in the 1983 United States Grand Prix West at Long Beach, California, has a place in the history books as the race in which the winner started from the lowest position on the grid.

And unless F1 expands its current field of 20 cars by another team, it will likely stay that way forever, for Watson remarkably came through the field to triumph from 22nd place on the grid.

It was Long Beach's final race as an F1 event. By 1983, founder and promoter Chris Pook was convinced the numbers were not adding up, and it switched to hosting IndyCars from 1984 for greater financial security.

Since then, it has transformed itself into what McLaren Racing boss Zak Brown calls "the Monaco of IndyCar". Back when Long Beach was a Formula 1 track, between 1977 and 1983, it lacked that cachet. Long Beach then was a mostly depressed port city. The race developed quite a reputation in those few years, but any elegance and allure came more from its proximity to the bright lights of Hollywood and Los Angeles than the location itself.

"It was the first street track in North America that F1 had raced on," Watson remembers. "It was very much a navy town. Not so much

dodgy, but it didn't have the polish and glamour of Hollywood.

"On the pit straight, there may have been a few little places, you might have called them dives. It had character, let's put it that way."

Long Beach started its life as a Formula 5000 race in 1976, switching to F1 in 1977, and it was a place where things tended to happen, both

good and bad. In 1979, it was the confirmation of Ferrari's arrival as the leading contender for what would be their final drivers' championship for 21 years. The winner that day, Gilles Villeneuve,

OPPOSITE: John Watson in the McLaren-Ford on the streets of Long Beach in 1983. In the distance, at top of the frame, is the RMS *Queen Mary*.

TOP: Gilles Villeneuve (27), starting from fifth on the grid, gets a flyer at the start of the 1981 race but then runs wide.

would not take the title, but teammate Jody Scheckter, who finished second, would.

In 1980, it witnessed the awful end to the distinguished career of one of the leading drivers of the 1970s, Clay Regazzoni, when he crashed his Ensign at the end of the track's long, curving straight, Shoreline Drive. Brake failure on the car sent it head-on into the barriers, the impact breaking his spine and leaving the Swiss paralyzed.

In 1982, the track marked the first win of Niki Lauda's return to Formula 1 with McLaren, which climaxed with his third world title two years later.

And then came Watson's win in 1983. Ask him how on earth he won from so far back, and 'Wattie' starts by recalling how he had pulled out of a promotional tour of South America organised by his McLaren team's sponsor Marlboro, under pressure from the British media, who thought it was bad form so soon after the end of the Falklands War.

Lauda, though, did go, and that left Watson with the exclusive use of Lauda's trainer/physio/guru Willi Dungl, who had been employed to finely hone the Austrian's mind and body for his comeback.

Dungl's big thing, Watson says, was ensuring his drivers had the optimum blood-sugar ratio for their constitution, and he would test them

regularly and adjust their diet to fine-tune it. "I had Willi's undivided attention the week before and I thought that was fantastic. I had never been a part of this, and I felt it was extremely valuable."

The McLarens qualified so badly because the Michelin tyres they used were primarily designed for the turbo cars of Renault and Brabham. McLaren in 1983 were still using Cosworth engines, and the low-power, lightweight cars simply did not generate sufficient energy in the tyres on a low-fuel qualifying run to work the rubber up to the right temperature. Which meant no grip.

Fuelled up in the race, the extra energy from the added weight 'turned on' the tyres, and the nimble McLaren came into its own. The two cars, Lauda initially ahead after jumping Watson at the start, began to carve through the field as if the rest of their competitors were not there.

"Every time he made a pass, I stuck to him. I was his doppelgänger," Watson says. "Eventually, thanks also to drivers making mistakes and reliability, we went through the field until we were running third and fourth. I felt I had a chance to get ahead of him and the most likely place was into the right-left sequence at the end of Shoreline Drive.

"I did a fairly late move and got alongside him, the car flinched a bit towards him – I was so late on the brakes the front grabbed momentarily – but once I was ahead I was off and running."

That left only the Brabham of Riccardo Patrese and Jacques Laffite's Williams up ahead. Patrese retired from second place and Watson soon dispensed with the Williams and cruised on to the finish line.

It is Dungl to whom he credits the win. "Willi said afterwards: 'John, I knew you'd win the race.'

I think he saw something in me, which he had probably recognized at other races, in terms of my ability and capacity. It wasn't necessarily fully exploited or developed or whatever – partly down to me, partly down to McLaren, whatever.

"I had qualities that were different to Niki's but actually they were very strong and under-used and maybe even I didn't appreciate my own

RIGHT John Watson and Niki Lauda celebrate the unlikeliest podium in F1 history.

BELOW AND OPPOSITE: The Long Beach Grand Pix has continued to thrive with an IndyCar race as part of the IRL, while the neighbourhood has become considerably upscale.

potential or quality. But Willi did, and that was a very important moment for me."

Long Beach has witnessed much since. The track has gone through several layout changes, although the two famous defining straights of Shoreline Drive and Seaside Way have always been part of it, and the city itself, too.

The dive bars and condemned buildings have been replaced by high-rise hotels and tourist attractions, and it is a high point of the IndyCar season. But it is unlikely ever again to witness something as remarkable as Watson's win in March 1983.

Macau

Macau, China

Ask a Formula 1 driver to name their favourite circuit, and you will likely get a choice from a very small selection: Suzuka, Spa, Monaco, Silverstone. But they may well ask whether they can pick a track that does not hold a grand prix, and then they will add another into the mix, Macau.

Macau is in southern China, about an hour by jetfoil ferry from Hong Kong, and is host to one of the most remarkable circuits ever created.

Formula 1 driver Carlos Sainz Junior volunteered it as a comparison when driving the high-speed Jeddah street circuit for the first time in 2021. "The intensity it gives you and the thrill and adrenaline is something I haven't lived since my Macau days," Sainz said. "Very high speed, very intense, very close to the walls trying to get the turning points right, it is quite crazy."

The Macau Grand Prix, held every November, is unique in being the only high-level event in the world where cars and motorcycles compete on the same track on the same weekend. There are races for bikes, touring cars and sportscars, while the centrepiece is the most prestigious Formula 3 event on the calendar.

Macau's Guia circuit is a 6.12km (3.80 mile) street track that is like Monaco crossed with Suzuka or Silverstone, and it is split into two distinct parts. First, there is a long main 'straight' – which actually has two flat-out kinks, first a left and then a right – where F3 cars can top 274km/h (170mph). This is ended by the notorious Lisboa corner, a 90-degree right

hander, where there always seems to be a multi-car pile-up, sometimes terrifying, such as 18-year-old Sophia Flörsch's horrifying airborne crash in the 2018 F3 race when the German driver broke her back. She has since made a full recovery and is back racing.

After that, the second half of the circuit is a switchback climb up and then back down the hill behind the sea front, the cars swooping left and right between barriers painted in Macau's trademark black and yellow. It is uphill until the evocatively named Solitude Esses, before it starts to wind downhill again back to the sea front.

It is high speed, demands extreme precision and is quite simply one of the most demanding pieces of race track in the world. It ends with the tightest point on the track, the Melco Hairpin, which is just 7 metres (23 ft) wide. Because of this combination of extreme claustrophobia and high levels of difficulty, Macau is a place where things happen, and where drivers do extraordinary things.

Most famously, perhaps, it is the place where the world first saw the extreme and dubious tactics that Michael Schumacher was prepared to utilise in pursuit of Formula 1 victory.

In 1991, the race was run over two heats. Schumacher was leading the second heat, and Mika Häkkinen was right behind him. Having won the first heat, Häkkinen had to sit behind Schumacher for only 2 seconds to be declared the overall winner. Häkkinen found himself with a perfect tow, and he couldn't resist the temptation of trying to pass.

TOP: Mika Häkkinen (2) heads Michael Schumacher (3) in what the *South China Morning Post* described as the most memorable Macau Grand Prix of all time.

ABOVE: 18-year-old Sebastián Montoya – son of Juan Pablo Montoya – rounds the Melco Hairpin, one of the tightest turns in international motorsport.

OPPOSITE: Pepe Martí in the Red Bull-sponsored Campos Racing car on his way to fifth place in the feature race.

Schumacher, watching the Finn closely in his mirrors, jinked right very late, and Häkkinen clipped the back of his car and crashed. Schumacher continued to victory.

Fast forward nine years and the German tried a similar trick as they contested victory in the 2000 Belgian Grand Prix, edging Häkkinen onto the grass at 322km/h (200mph) with a late move, The next lap, Häkkinen passed Schumacher in his now famous overtake where the sparring drivers went either side of backmarker Ricardo Zonta's BAR and the Finn ending in front. Afterwards, Häkkinen had a tense talk with his rival in the pit lane, using hand gestures to show how close they had come to disaster and making it clear he expected Schumacher never to try such tactics again.

Alongside Schumacher, other notable winners of Macau include Ayrton Senna, David Coulthard and two-time Indianapolis 500 winner Takuma Sato. But Macau is also a place where failures can be as heroic as successes, and where great drivers can do great things that sometimes overshadow the overall winner. One such example was in 1994. Dane Jan Magnussen (father of Kevin) arrived in Macau as hot favourite.

Driving for Paul Stewart Racing, he had dominated the British F3 championship, his 14 wins in 18 races breaking Senna's 21-year-old record. But Magnussen crashed at the right-hander of Moorish Bend during qualifying and lined up 18th on the grid. It set the stage for a remarkable comeback. By the end of the first race, he was fifth, and he won the second, to be classified third overall behind winner Sascha Maassen and the Dane's PSR team-mate Kelvin Burt.

A very similar performance came from a certain Max Verstappen 20 years later on his sole appearance at Macau in 2014, not long after the Dutchman had made his F1 debut with a run in free practice at Suzuka.

Verstappen was quickly up to second in the qualifying race but wouldn't settle for that. In a bid for the lead, he crashed at the Solitude Esses, sending him to the back for the main race. His team boss Frits van Amersfoort remembers his frustration: "If you finish P2 in the qualifying race in Macau, it is more value than being on pole in the feature race because in Macau you don't want to be on pole, then you are a target for everyone behind you (with the slipstream). And that's Max.

"And the other side was in the feature race on Sunday. There was this pile-up, like usual in Macau, and Max's car was badly damaged. There was only one way to continue and that was to get back to the pits to the start grid. But all the marshals told him to get out of the car because they wanted to tow it away. He stayed in the car and refused to get out. He was somewhere hanging (on a crane) and as soon as they put him on the road, he started the car and drove back on three wheels to the grid, and we were

able to repair the car. And in the end he finished seventh, coming from the back.

"This incredible drive, this incredible internal will to win, I haven't seen anything like that before and I've seen a lot of race drivers."

OPPOSITE TOP: German teenager Sophia Flörsch's car was launched into the catch-fencing at Turn 3 in a frightening accident in 2018. After back surgery she made a full recovery, returned to racing and placed 11th in the 2023 Macau GP.

OPPOSITE BOTTOM: Pepe Martí on track during the Sunday feature race.

ABOVE: Sebastián Montoya rounds Turn 3, Lisboa, one of the biggest stops in the race and a natural overtaking point.

Madras International Circuit

Irungattukottai, Chennai, India

For many years, India's original motor racing circuit, completed in 1989, had a singularly exotic reputation among those few international competitors fortunate enough to have experienced it. The pits were made from cow sheds, their roofs were made of asbestos. And before they went out to compete, drivers were warned not to get out of their cars should they go off the track and onto the infield. The run-off areas were grass, and in them were snakes – poisonous ones. If you were really unlucky, it could even be a cobra. Best to stay in the car and wait for the marshals.

Things have moved on since those early days – in the early 2010s the track underwent a major renovation. Where once there were cow sheds, now there is a modern pit building. The snakes are still there, but are less of a concern now that the run-off areas are gravel.

The Madras International Circuit still has its wild edge, though. The track is surrounded by drainage channels, which cars sometimes reach if the accident is big enough. Small crocodiles make them their home – only two or three feet long, but enough to give anyone a fright.

Broadcaster and racing driver Karun Chandhok tells a story about when he was running a team in 2006. One of his drivers headed off down the pit lane, only to stop the car and jump out with the engine still running and sprint away. A snake had crawled up from the pedal box between his legs as he set off.

The track was the brainchild of Chandhok's grandfather, Bharat Indu Chandhok, and his friends S. Muthukrishnan and V. Chidambaram.

They had founded the Madras Motor Club but grew tired of racing on tracks built from former airfields whose surface was also used for testing tanks. Chandhok and his friends were well connected – one of the club members was an Indian movie star called M. G. Ramachandran, who had moved on to become the chief minister of the state of Tamil Nadu.

Still buying the land was not a quick or easy process. The club purchased just over 300 hectares of land that was being used as padi fields. There were hundreds of owners, who had to be bused in, 50 or so at a time, to a register office to satisfy Indian bureaucracy.

Jackie Stewart laid the foundation stone, the track was built by Larsen & Toubro, India's biggest contractor, and it has held international motor races ever since, starting with the Madras Formula 3 Grand Prix from 1991–94, and moving on to touring cars, Porsche Supercup and others.

More than 40 years on, it remains one of only two international standard tracks in India and is in use for more than 300 days a year for races and manufacturer testing.

The track still retains its charm, despite its modernization. The pits have been rebuilt, there is a race control building and even hospitality suites. "It is less of a jungle," Chandhok says, "but the rustic feel is still there".

OPPOSITE: Brazilian driver Felipe Drugovich, Aston Martin's 2024 reserve and test driver, in action at Madras in 2017.

LEFT: Driver briefings at the Madras circuit contain an element not deemed necessary at Snetterton or Cadwell Park.

Marina Bay Circuit

Marina Bay, Singapore

The Singapore Grand Prix was the first Formula 1 night race and has become one of the most financially important events on the calendar. It is also a brutally demanding test of man and machine.

The race at Marina Bay is one of the highlights of the F1 season. The key to the event's ground-breaking success was to hold the race after dark in one of the world's most impressive locations.

The cars glisten under about 1,600 custom-made lights illuminating the track. The circuit is lined with large, Chinese-style lanterns. Colonial buildings adorn the perimeter and Singapore's skyline provides a futuristic *Blade Runner*-style backdrop.

As the sun sets across the Singapore Strait, and the lights around the track are switched on, the whole city seems to sparkle, providing an evocative build-up to qualifying and race. The occasional intrusion onto the track of one of Singapore's population of sizeable monitor lizards only adds to the quirky appeal.

Singapore has always had a certain cachet. It's a place where the old world meets the new, the nineteenth-century class of the Raffles Hotel combining with modern attractions such as the Gardens By The Bay, and the towers of the Marina Bay Sands hotel. It's easy to see why it has became one of the most glamorous and sought-after events in Formula 1.

For the drivers, too, Singapore has an allure. They appreciate all the above, but for them there is one additional feature.

OPPOSITE: The Singapore night race was a revelation – for the first time an East Asian grand prix could be transmitted at a convenient time to its core audience in Europe.

TOP: Race leader Felipe Massa sets off from his pit box in 2008 with the refuelling hose still attached. Without the botched stop he could have been World Champion.

ABOVE: Fernando Alonso was pitted for tyres extraordinarily early in 2008. And then his teammate crashed…

This is the place where they are tested to their absolute limit by the combination of tropical heat and humidity, the bumpy track and the longest grand prix on the calendar. The Marina Bay circuit is one of the slowest on the calendar, but that is exactly why the race is so tough. It means the minimum 305km (190 mile) grand prix distance runs to nearly two hours.

This is the race at which all the drivers' intensive physical preparations are targeted. Ferrari's Carlos Sainz says "When I'm training in pre-season, January and February, I'm not thinking about the first race, I'm thinking about Singapore. If you survive Singapore, then you're fit for anything else in Formula 1."

What appears to be merely a collection of mostly right-angled corners is actually a deceptively challenging, technical layout with significant variety, lined with concrete walls to catch the unwary. It's not by chance that two of the defining qualifying laps of the modern era were both done in Singapore – by Lewis Hamilton for Mercedes in 2018 and Charles Leclerc in his Ferrari the following year. In both cases, the commitment and skill on show as the drivers took their cars to the absolute limit and flirted with the circuit limits was awe-inspiring.

Marina Bay has had two main configurations. The first one was 5.07km (3.14 miles) long, and the only change over the first 13 events was for the 2013 event. This involved the easing of a particularly awkward and tight chicane at Turn 10, the so-called Singapore Sling, to make a more flowing left-handed turn.

ABOVE LEFT: Sebastian Vettel puts a dent in his 2017 championship ambitions by swerving in front of Max Verstappen and then collecting the Ferrari of his teammate, Kimi Raikkonen.

LEFT: Singapore is indeed the home of F1 night racing, and also the venue that tests drivers' physical resilience to the maximum.

OPPOSITE: The success of the grand prix has allowed Formula 1 to replicate the event with more night races, and helped make a Las Vegas GP a reality.

The second iteration was first used in 2023, cutting out the left-right-right-left combination where the track went under a grandstand late in the lap, as a result of redevelopment works, removing four corners and shortening the lap to 4.94km (3.07 miles).

The initial intention was to revert to the original layout once the building work was complete, but the drivers almost unanimously agreed that the changes improved the flow of the track while maintaining its character. Once the work is completed, likely around 2026–27, the track will be reconfigured to suit the redeveloped area.

The demanding nature of Marina Bay creates races with a particular signature. This is the only event on the calendar where there has been a safety car at every single event.

Races tend to be slowburn and defined by hectic action around pit stops, and sometimes at the end as different strategies bring cars with varying tyre life together, as happened in 2023. Sainz found himself holding off a train of three other cars – McLaren's Lando Norris and Mercedes drivers George Russell and Lewis Hamilton – in reverse pace order. This led to the most dramatic last lap in Singapore's history, when Norris brushed the wall at Turn 10, Russell hit it properly and crashed right behind him, and Sainz held on for the only non-Red Bull victory of the year.

One race, though, has come to overshadow all others at Singapore: the first one. This was the infamous 'crash-gate' race, when Renault driver Nelson Piquet Jr's early crash played into the hands of teammate Fernando Alonso, who had just made a pit stop, and vaulted up the order as everyone else pitted under the safety car put out while Piquet's car was recovered.

Alonso went on to win the race, after a couple of other events played into his hands, most notably

Ferrari bungling leader Felipe Massa's stop under the safety car and sending the Brazilian on his way with the fuel hose still attached to his car.

There were immediate suspicions that something was not right, but it was only a year later when Piquet said publicly that he had been asked to crash by his team and an inquiry was instigated by governing body the FIA that the facts were revealed.

Renault team boss Flavio Briatore and chief technical officer Pat Symonds were given

temporary bans from the sport for orchestrating a deliberate crash with the aim of manipulating the race. Alonso has always denied any prior knowledge of the plans, and the inquiry cleared him, but within Formula 1 there remains scepticism about that to this day.

Mille Miglia

Brescia, Italy

Few motorsport events are as iconic as the Mille Miglia, or have packed so many celebrated stories into a relatively short lifespan.

First staged in 1927, the Mille Miglia literally translates as "1,000 miles". And that's exactly what it was: a 1,000-mile race (1600km) around Italy. Of course, like so many corner names at Italian circuits, it sounds all the more romantic in its native tongue.

When staged competitively, the Mille Miglia was a roughly figure-of-eight route from Brescia just to the west of Lake Garda, to Rome and back again. There have been many different versions of the route, but all share the characteristics of a race on normal roads, past towns and villages and over mountains, through the very heart of Italy. It has come to be regarded as the archetypal Italian road race – the older Targa Florio notwithstanding – one event that

encapsulates an era and a country's relationship with a sport. So much so that only three times in its 30-year competitive existence has it been won by a foreigner in a non-Italian car.

One of those times, the 1955 staging, is the definitive edition of the event. Stirling Moss won it in a Mercedes 300 SLR, effectively the company's Formula 1 car of that year lightly modified so it could be driven on normal roads and from day into night.

Moss overcame his lack of knowledge of the local roads by getting his co-driver, the idiosyncratic British motorsport journalist Denis Jenkinson, to write pace notes. The pair completed six tours of that year's route, and Jenkinson wrote his notes onto an 18-foot length of paper that was on two rollers in a box on his lap, and communicated with Moss with hand signals, as they could not hear each other over the sound from the Mercedes's V8 engine.

In what has become acknowledged as one of Moss's greatest ever performances, the pair competed the course in an all-time record of 10 hours 7 minutes and 48 seconds, with an average speed of 157.65km/h (97.96mph).

OPPOSITE: Stirling Moss with navigator Denis Jenkinson in their Mercedes 300 SLR en route to victory in 1955.

LEFT: Juan Manuel Fangio in his Mercedes 300 SLR on the starting ramp in Brescia for the 22nd running of the Mille Miglia, in 1955.

Those numbers would be remarkable enough at the time had they been achieved on a race track. But these were public roads, through Verona, to Ravenna, heading south on the Adriatic coast before turning inland at Pescara across the Apennines to Rome and then north through Sienna, Florence, Modena and back to Brescia.

It's a mind-boggling achievement, incredibly brave, but even Moss acknowledged the risks involved. As he put it many years later: "Imagine going up a large incline towards a village and going at 185 miles (298km/h) per hour without knowing which way the road goes. It was the only race that frightened me, actually."

Moss was not done after winning the Mille Miglia. He attended the after-party, left Brescia just after midnight and drove through the night with his girlfriend Sally Weston in his Mercedes 200 saloon to breakfast in Munich, and then on to Mercedes HQ in Stuttgart by noon.

He had lunch with directors, had new seats fitted to his car, left at 5.15pm, arrived in Cologne at 9.15pm, where he finally checked into a hotel. He had been awake – behind the wheel for much of the time – for at least 40 hours.

Remarkable as Moss's achievement was, it is just one of many incredible feats on the Mille Miglia. That same year, his Mercedes teammate Juan Manuel Fangio did something just as spectacular. The Argentine finished second, also completing the course in less than 11 hours, and just half an hour behind Moss, despite driving solo, hitting engine problems at Pescara, and running on

TOP: A scene from the 2023 *Ferrari* movie which depicts the 1957 Mille Miglia won by car no.535, Piero Taruffi, in a Ferrari 315S.

LEFT: Today, the Mille Miglia lives on through classic re-runs along the route.

OPPOSITE: Cars stop off in the famous Piazza del Campo in Siena for the 2023 recreation of the event.

seven cylinders from Florence after an injection pipe broke.

Then there was the 1930 race – a duel between the two greatest Italian racers of the inter-war period, Tazio Nuvolari and Achille Varzi. Teammates in Alfa Romeo 6Cs, Varzi was running ahead (Nuvolari had started behind him in the one-by-one order and was ahead on time by 10 minutes) but suspected his hopes of victory were over when he saw Nuvolari's headlights behind him in the closing stages of the race.

But then the lights disappeared and Varzi began to believe he might win after all... until 10 miles from the finish. He was awoken from his reverie by a flash of headlights and a blast of the horn. Nuvolari had been sitting on his tail, following him through the mountains, lights off. Measures of respect don't come much higher than that.

Either side of Moss's win, there were other dazzling drives. In 1954, 1956 and 1957,

Alberto Ascari, Eugenio Castellotti and Piero Taruffi all won driving solo. Taruffi's win was the last. The Mille Miglia already had a reputation as one of the most dangerous motorsport events, as spectators, including children, crowded the roadsides trying to catch a glimpse of the fastest sportscars and drivers of the day.

In 1957, Castellotti had been killed testing a Ferrari at Monza just weeks before the Mille Miglia, and then, just a few miles from the finish, Spanish nobleman Alfonso de Portago, Taruffi's Ferrari teammate, suffered a puncture at speed. His car flipped and smashed into spectators standing by the side of the road. In addition to De Portago and his co-driver Edmund Nelson, nine spectators were killed, five of them children.

In Italy, there was outcry. The public demanded justice, and Enzo Ferrari was put on trial for manslaughter. Taruffi, whose final race it was, wrote an article that was published by the American magazine the *Saturday Evening Post*.

It was titled: 'Stop Us Before We Kill Again.' It was a plea for open-road races like the Mille Miglia to "be put to death".

"It was Le Mans all over again," Taruffi wrote. "I tried to look as a victor should look, but in my heart there was only despair, for I realised that the Mille Miglia had become too dangerous and that I must be one of its pallbearers."

Ferrari was eventually acquitted, with the accident blamed on cats' eyes in the road. But it was the end for the Mille Miglia as a competitive race. In 1977 it was reborn as a regularity rally – an event in which time and average speed are the determining factors, not absolute pace. The cars allowed to compete are historic models that were registered no later than 1957 and had attended the original race.

The Targa Florio, the last of these types of events, continued until 1977 in Sicily, but essentially the last Mille Miglia marked the beginnings of the modern age of motorsport, when safety was paramount, and the end of a time in which death was considered merely an unfortunate consequence. Even so, it took another decade, and Jackie Stewart's intervention, for that concept to become crystallized as a movement that could no longer be resisted.

OPPOSITE: Only models of cars that competed in the original Mille Miglia, up to 1957, are eligible for the classic re-runs.

BELOW LEFT: Former McLaren-Mercedes driver Mika Häkkinen got to drive the Fangio 300 SLR on the Bologna-Roma stage in 2011.

BELOW: A police officer guides a classic BMW through the narrow streets of Siena.

Milwaukee Mile

West Allis, Wisconsin, USA

The Milwaukee Mile is the oldest race track in the world. This one-mile oval in Wisconsin State Fair Park has held at least one race every year since 1903, other than during the USA's participation in World War II.

Originally a dirt-track course, like so many circuits in the US, the Mile was paved in 1954 and held the country's two leading championships, NASCAR and IndyCar, for many years until running into difficulties early this century.

Traditionally, the Mile was the first race held in the IndyCar calendar after the Indianapolis 500. It says something that it managed to carve a strong reputation despite constantly being in the shadow of one of the world's biggest races – the Indy 500 is such an attention focus in American motorsport that it tends to suck the spotlight away from anything anywhere near it.

A classic oval, two straights joined by two long, banked corners, the Milwaukee Mile developed a reputation for great racing. American legend Rick Mears, a four-time Indy 500 winner, took three victories there and says one of its secrets was the shallow nine-degree banking – the same angle as the Indy 500, but relatively low for such a short track.

"Milwaukee offered more options in terms of what you could do with the placement of the car," he said, explaining that the corners enabled drivers to experiment with lines as the fuel load came off and the tyres wore. The more skilled ones could take advantage of the need to extemporize.

Perhaps it owes its status to longevity, and the fact that it had an NFL stadium in the middle of the oval, hosting the Green Bay Packers from 1934–51. But the Milwaukee Mile has also been central to some major historical events in motorsport.

In 1963, Jim Clark took the first IndyCar win for a rear-engined car in his Lotus, a couple of months after being denied the same in a controversial Indy 500, in which he finished second to Parnelli Jones. Many observers thought Clark was the rightful victor at Indy. Jones's car was dropping oil for many laps, and caused at least one other car to crash. It was felt that if an American car had been behind Jones, rather than Clark in the upstart Lotus, it would have black-flagged.

Still, Clark and Lotus returned to Indy to finish the job the following year, and their success was the beginning of the end for front-engined roadsters in IndyCar.

Legends Mario Andretti and Gordon Johncock both took their first oval wins at Milwaukee: Johncock in 1965 and Andretti in 1966. And in 1991, Mario and his sons Michael and John made racing history by becoming the first – and still only – family to finish first, second and third in any motorsport event in the world. Michael won, with John second and Mario third.

As the 2000s progressed, organisers at the Mile found it increasingly difficult to market events there and make them pay, and both IndyCars and the premier NASCAR series stopped visiting in 2010s.

But it returned to the IndyCar calendar in 2024 in a deal brokered by Roger Penske, US motorsport titan and owner of the Indianapolis Motor Speedway. Penske, a renowned business genius with a wide-reaching empire in the US, is confident he can make it work financially, so there is hope that this historic track can have a new lease of life in contemporary times.

OPPOSITE: Colby Howard (9) leads Rajah Caruth and Conner Jones during the Clean Harbors 175, part of the NASCAR Craftsman Truck Series, in August 2023.

BELOW: Like so many other US circuits, Milwaukee started off as a dirt track.

Monte Carlo Rally

Monaco

If you like motorsport, and perhaps even cycling, the chances are you will have heard of the Col de Turini. A mountain pass in the Alps Maritime, the Turini is the centrepiece of the most famous rally in the world, the Monte Carlo. And an occasional stage of the Tour de France, too.

It's also a route that the many F1 drivers who choose Monaco as their home often find themselves cycling up on training rides. But that's merely an interesting footnote to the presence of this sinuous piece of asphalt on the Principality's other blue riband motorsport event.

First held in 1911, and run pretty much annually ever since, the Monte Carlo Rally is, as two-time world rally champion Carlos Sainz says: "For every single driver, the priority."

The Col de Turini is a 31km (19 mile) route that runs from La Bollène to Vésubie, or sometimes the other way around, at an average gradient of 6.7%. It's steep and has many hairpins. It's driven at night, in January, and to make things more difficult, some of the many spectators who line the route throw snow and ice on to the road.

What makes the Monte Carlo Rally so difficult beyond the serpentine nature of the roads is that drivers are never quite sure what surface they will encounter. Will it be dry asphalt? Wet asphalt? Will there be snow and ice? If so, how much?

"In the past," Sainz says, "it used to be the last night when the rally was more or less decided around the Alps close to Monaco. Sometimes now it is more at the beginning of the rally.

"This stage goes up to 1,400m (4,593 ft) so it could be on many occasions the last two kilometres of the col and the first two going down that are with ice and snow. It could be a completely dry stage or it could be very challenging depending on how much snow there is that year.

"Many times you have part of the stage with some ice or snow but basically many kilometres it is more for slicks. Then the biggest challenge is to choose the correct tyre."

This is much harder than it sounds. There might only be three or four kilometres of ice compared to 25km (16 miles) of asphalt, but that can be enough to force a driver to choose studded ice tyres. Less ice than that, but still some, and you might want slicks with circumferential grooves cut into them.

"Sometimes it could be as much as 40–45 seconds per kilometre difference between a studded tyre and a kind of slick," Sainz says.

But the Monte Carlo is not just about one stage. There are many just as difficult. "The Turini is a nice stage," he says, "but in my opinion there were other stages more challenging. For example, Sisteron used to be a decider stage and the last part of the stage used to be always with some ice. And difficult, more narrow than Turini."

Really, though, the Monte Carlo is famous because the entire event is special. "It's unique," says Sainz "and, depending on the weather and conditions, it can be incredibly challenging."

ABOVE: A Renault Alpine competing in the classic version of the event.

OPPOSITE: Red Bull-sponsored driver Adrien Fourmaux on the road section near Gap in Southern France. Fourmaux and Alexandre Coria took their Ford Puma Rally to fifth place in 2024.

Norisring

Nuremberg, Germany

The Norisring in the German city of Nuremberg has one of the most unusual features of any race track in the world; It is a temporary street circuit in a park just outside the city centre, remarkable not for its simple layout but for its backdrop.

The main grandstand opposite the pits – the Steintribune – was first constructed by the Nazis to hold the infamous Nuremberg rallies in the 1930s, when thousands of members of the National Socialist Party gathered in uniform to hear Adolf Hitler's deranged speeches.

The area was badly damaged by bombing in World War II, but the grandstand, also known as the Zeppelinhaupttribüne, remains more or less intact, and was transformed into a 25,000-seat grandstand for the first race at the track in 1948. Nowadays, spectators flock to Nuremberg for the annual race at the Norisring for the DTM, or German Touring Car Championship, a huge crowd-puller in the country.

In quieter times, a walk to the top of the grandstand, looking over where the mass of Nazis would assemble in the 1930s, is a sobering experience and a reminder of one of the darkest periods of human history.

On race weekends, however, the place takes on a different atmosphere – one of celebration. Copious amounts of Pilsner and Weissbier bier are drunk as fans enjoy the festivities.

The track is just 2.30km (1.42 miles) long and consists of a main straight into a tight hairpin, which takes the cars back up the other side of the same road, and then into a 90-degree right-left combination – the Scholler 'S' – another

straight up the other side of the main grandstand before a second hairpin turns back onto the pit straight. Simple – almost simplistic.

Why is it called the Norisring? The name, acquired in 1950 after a competition, harks back to an old moniker for the city – Noris. It was adopted in the hope of avoiding confusion with the rather more famous Nürburgring circuit in the Eifel mountains (see page 158).

The Norisring has one more unfortunate claim to fame, and this one, too, is tinged with tragedy. It is the place where the leading Mexican F1 and sportscar driver Pedro Rodríguez lost his life in 1971.

He crashed his Porsche 917 on what was then a longer run from the first hairpin towards the Scholler 'S', and he died in the subsequent fire. The track was shortened afterwards to reduce corner approach speeds.

OPPOSITE: A packed grid for the DTM race and equally packed grandstands making use of the old neoclassical tribune.

BELOW LEFT: The track has a chequered past – it was the host of numerous Nazi rallies during World War II. The site was also used as a Zeppelin field.

BELOW: An aerial view of the DTM pack as it negotiates a door-handle-removing opening lap in 2023.

Nürburgring

Nürburg, Rhineland-Palatinate, Germany

The greatest race circuit ever built last hosted Formula 1 in 1976, and John Watson was there for the two key incidents that sounded the death knell for elite level motorsport at the Nürburgring Nordschleife.

The first was Niki Lauda's near-fatal accident on the second lap of that year's German Grand Prix.

The race had nearly been cancelled on safety grounds – Lauda, the reigning world champion, had tried to organise a boycott, but the drivers narrowly voted against.

Lauda's objection was that it was impossible to bring a lap of over 22km (14 miles) – with 170-odd corners, fast and narrow, winding and twisting around the Eifel mountains, rising and falling with 300m (984 ft) of elevation – up to the safety standards of the day. His point applied to safety of the track's infrastructure, such as barriers, but also to the number of marshals and access by medical teams around such a long lap.

So it was a terrible irony that it was Lauda who crashed horribly at a fast, left-hand kink before a right-hander called Bergwerk. His Ferrari snapped to the right and bounced off an earth bank back into the middle of the track, where it was nudged by Brett Lunger's Surtees.

When Watson arrived on the scene a few seconds later in his Penske, fellow driver Arturo Merzario was standing on the sidepods of Lauda's Ferrari trying to drag him out of the car.

"I stopped my car, got out, and went down to the scene," Watson recalls. "Niki had just been taken out of the car and there was a lot of fluid

on the track and I didn't know whether from the radiators or fuel or whatever, so I said: 'Let's bring him back up towards my car,' to a bit of the race track that was dry.

"He walked up, assisted, and he was lucid in a very shocked way. And I said: 'I am going to

OPPOSITE: Juan Manuel Fangio, Maserati 250F (left) and Mike Hawthorn, Lancia-Ferrari 801 (right)– two of the three protagonists in 'the greatest race in F1 history', the 1957 German Grand Prix.

BELOW: Niki Lauda stands by the side of his Ferrari 312T2 as it is refuelled during practice.

BELOW RIGHT: The start of the fateful 1976 grand prix.

RIGHT: John Watson with team boss Roger Penske in 1976.

kneel down. Lie down on the race track, put your head on my thigh and the medical service will be here in a minute.'

"I was looking down at him, and I could see that his scalp was very, very badly burned. He said: 'What's my face look like?'

"I had never seen anybody who had been burned before, but I was aware I could see his forehead and he had lost skin.

"I said: 'No, you're fine, don't worry about it. They'll be here in a minute, you're going to be fine.' I was just trying to keep him distracted and whatever you would do in those circumstances to help him.

"He was conscious but clearly deeply shocked. He was aware he had been in a fire, he was aware he had suffered burns. He didn't know the extent of them but what's the point of telling him?"

The extent of them was that Lauda, with third-degree burns and lungs damaged by the fire, was taken to hospital, where he was given the last rites by a local priest. But just 40 days later, he was back at the wheel of his Ferrari in the Italian Grand Prix, still-raw wounds protected by bandages under his helmet.

Lauda's crash is widely remembered as the reason the Nordschleife finally lost its place on the F1 calendar, after nearly 50 years of building up a reputation as the most fearsome, demanding, yet rewarding race track on earth.

The legend was partly true. But this being F1, it was not quite as straightforward as that. In 1977, safety at the Nürburgring was still very much a concern, but the track was on the calendar in the early part of the year.

Bernie Ecclestone, boss of the Brabham team, was also running the commercial side of F1

and could see that a 22.5km (14 mile) track was not the ideal scenario in the dawning television age. He had other ideas for the location of the German Grand Prix.

In 1977, Watson was driving for Brabham and Lauda was poised to join the team for the following season after falling out with Enzo Ferrari because of the way he had behaved following the Austrian's accident.

Watson says: "The reason it came off after Niki's accident was because in 1977 Bernie said to me: 'I want you and Niki to go to Nürburgring and do a track inspection, because I have a deal with Hockenheim.' And the reason it was taken off the calendar is that Niki and I went there and said: 'It's no longer appropriate.'"

Was that what Ecclestone wanted them both to say or did they really believe it?

"It was a little bit of both," Watson says. "The reality was that a grand prix of 14 laps isn't a great television spectacle. Secondly, the potential for circuit advertising was developing and a circuit of that distance isn't going to be profitable in terms of putting circuit advertising other than bits down the start-finish straight and whatever.

"So, from Bernie's commercial perspective, representing the Formula One Constructors' Association (FOCA), Hockenheim was a total no-brainer."

Nearly 50 years later, Watson, now in his late 70s, can still talk you around a lap of the Nordschleife, still remember the famous corner names – Flugplatz, Fuchs Rohre (Fox Hole), Adenau Bridge, Breidscheid, Karussell, Pflanzgarten and so on.

The pull of the place is why, for some purists at the time, the idea of it no longer hosting

TOP: Cars line up for the start of the 1964 race. Because of the length of lap, organisers would sometimes add Formula 2 cars to the grid.

ABOVE: John Surtees (Ferrari) leads Jim Clark (Lotus) through the 'Green Hell' in the 1963 race.

OPPOSITE: Formula 1 last visited the reconfigured Nürburgring for the Eifel Grand Prix in 2020, but the modern circuit bears no resemblance to the Nordschleife.

F1 was so controversial. The Nürburgring had a hallowed status. Hockenheim was short of redeeming features, and it also had a reputation for danger. The great Jim Clark was killed there in an F2 race in 1968 when his Lotus speared off the road almost certainly as a result of tyre failure and plunged into the forest.

The Nordschleife's reputation had been carved the authentic way, through the force of history, and the great events that had happened there. Its legendary status burnished the reputations of generations of the world's leading drivers.

In the 1935 German Grand Prix, Tazio Nuvolari, arguably the greatest driver of the first half of the twentieth century, took his most celebrated victory when, in wet conditions and after a botched pit stop, he rejoined in sixth place in his Alfa Romeo Tipo B and caught and passed all the cars of the dominant Mercedes and Auto Union teams ahead of him. The fact that his win displeased the visiting Nazi hierarchy only added to the potency of the day.

In 1957, Juan Manuel Fangio clinched his fifth and final world title with a remarkably similar drive in a Maserati 250F, this time in the dry. He, too, suffered a botched pit stop, rejoining in third place, 48 seconds behind the Ferraris of Mike Hawthorn and Peter Collins, with nine laps to go. In the next 10 laps, he broke the lap record nine times, and passed both Collins and Hawthorn in the course of the penultimate lap. "I have never driven that quickly before in my life," Fangio said after the race, "and I don't think I will ever be able to do it again".

Later in life, he recognized the importance of the Nürburgring in the status of his victory. "That day I conquered it," he said. "On another day, perhaps it would have conquered me."

In 1968, it was Jackie Stewart's turn. Three months after Jim Clark's death, Stewart cemented his place as his countryman's successor as the greatest F1 driver, winning

by 4 minutes in his Tyrrell-run Matra on hand-cut tyres in atrociously wet and foggy conditions.

Even then, Stewart, the man who led the safety crusade of the late 1960s and early 1970s, was expressing his misgivings about the Nordschleife. After that drive in 1968, he dubbed it "The Green Hell" – a nickname that has stuck – and from then on said it was an anachronism even in the brutal and so often fatal era of the time.

After Lauda's accident, the fastest cars to race there were world endurance sports prototypes. But by 1983, even they felt it was a step too far. Stefan Bellof set the pole for that final race in his Porsche 956 with a lap in 6 minutes 11.13 seconds. Once prototypes had left the Nordschleife behind, the fastest cars to compete there were GT racers and Bellof's lap time grew ever more remote.

But then, in late 2017, Porsche had an idea. After three consecutive World Endurance Championship wins with their hybrid-engined 919, they decided to produce an 'Evo' version of the car, free of rules – stripped back, lightened, more power, special tyres – and go after lap records at the world's two most iconic circuits in 2018.

Timo Bernhard was the designated driver, and after beating the then-fastest F1 lap time at Spa-Francorchamps, Porsche set its sights on the Nürburgring. World endurance champion in 2015 and 2017, Bernhard is a Nordschleife specialist, who first drove sections of the track as a child, long before he had a driving licence, and then learned it in GT cars early in his career.

The idea was raised with Bernhard in a matter-of-fact style, and it took a while for the enormity of what he was about to do to sink in.

"I was never actually officially asked," he recalls. "They said: 'We are going to do this 919 tribute tour and one of the events will be the Nordschleife. You will be in the simulator and then you are going to do it'."

On his way home from Porsche in Weissach, there was a sudden realisation and a sharp intake of breath: "'Okay. It's going to be very fast.' It was the first time I thought about it more intensely and I understood the dimension of it, speed-wise and everything.

"Normally there are only four people running the simulator in the back office but the first time we were on the simulator and we ran the Nordschleife lap with the 919 Evo, I looked around and in this one office there were probably 20–25 people, because everybody wanted to watch the lap.

"I told them: 'Okay, you saw me have a crash in the middle of the session, and you see the speed.' I said: 'This is serious. It's not like Bahrain or Hockenheim or other places. You go there, you have no run-off, you have bumps, crests, high kerbs like the 1980s, you cannot just go there and try it out. You need to have a plan.'"

There were times, he admits, when he wondered what on earth he was doing.

"In a way, I was proud to be chosen," Bernhard says, "but I also felt the tension, because everybody knew it was going to be really tough. That it's dangerous, it's something unique. A lot of people will watch it.

"Not everybody liked the idea because of Stefan Bellof. He's still a hero in Germany, and we tried to put it into perspective as well because I was a Bellof fan myself. It was not something to measure the car or myself against him. It was more to showcase what nowadays was possible. So it was quite some pressure.

"Every possible corner that could be designed is combined in one track. You will find it on the Nordschleife. You have slow speed, high speed, mid-speed. On camber, off camber. Blind entries. You have crests, compressions.

"You have, I call them 3D corners because you arrive and you have to turn at an angle and then you have to do a direction change and it is up the hill, and the exit is off-cambered and you are sideways. Everything is there."

Preparation for the run was intense, but finally the day came. A run to check the systems, not fast. A familiarisation run with a new set of tyres, and then one lap with special tyres.

"This was already the record, like a 5:24," Bernhard says, "and basically that's when they wanted to stop already. But I could convince our team boss Andreas Seidl together with our technical director that I would like to do one more set-up change and then kind of another run to clean it up.

"He agreed but said: 'Okay, guys, don't mess it up.' Because we knew it was a challenging thing. And then I did the 5:19.546.

"Then we both knew, the race engineer and myself, once I crossed the start-finish line, when I went off throttle, straight away he was on the radio, saying: 'Yeah, I think we pack up.' We both agreed it was too much stress to do another lap."

That lap equated to a remarkable 233.8km/h (145.3mph). He topped 330km/h (205mph) at various points in the lap. If you've driven

around the Nordschleife – and anyone can, for the princely sum of €30 – you'll know how incredible that sounds.

"The shape of the track, of the corners, and the length, this is from a different era," Bernhard says. "This you feel. They have really preserved it like that and still we are able to race there. This is something unique and it is something you understand quite quickly. This is what makes the Nordschleife so special. No other place on earth is like that."

OPPOSITE: Mario Andretti in the Gold Leaf Team Lotus 63 (4WD) gets airborne at the Flugplatz in the 1969 German Grand Prix.

ABOVE RIGHT: Bernhard on one of his record-shattering runs.

RIGHT: The record-breaking Porsche 919 hypercar on show at the Goodwood Festival of Speed.

Pikes Peak

Colorado, USA

Even in a book dedicated to extraordinary motorsport events and achievements, Pikes Peak stands out from the crowd. A 19.99km (12.42 mile) road up a Colorado mountain, ending at 4,305 metres (14,115 ft) above sea level, with precipitous drops and no rules. It is, as course record holder Romain Dumas describes, "completely, completely crazy". And as a result, it has captured the public imagination like few other events.

The course runs to the top of the most visited mountain summit in America. And the race,

a time trial for which the words "hill climb" are nowhere near sufficient, embraces the true pioneering spirit of the west – liberal in the extreme, risk-taking, self-reliant. If Clint Eastwood's man with no name had done motor racing, this is where he would have done it.

To give a sense of the extreme demands of Pikes Peak, Dumas tells a story about the time he beat the course record held at the time by his good friend Sébastien Loeb.

Loeb is a rally legend, the most successful WRC exponent of all time, a nine-time world champion, who has also competed on the Dakar Rally and various other motor racing events. In 2013 he was the first man to complete the Pikes Peak course in less than 9 minutes, in a Peugeot 208 Turbo 16. Five years later, Dumas smashed the record in an electric Volkswagen ID.R, becoming the first man to go under 8 minutes.

Dumas says: "We are neighbours. We live quite close to each other in Switzerland, and we are quite good friends. After I beat the record, (French newspaper) L'Equipe did a big article, face to face, the same questions, and Loeb said: 'I will never go back to beat the time, because it was the most stressful race I had in my career.'

"And I looked at him – for me, rally drivers are my heroes more than endurance or F1 drivers or whatever – and I said: 'When you are in Finland or Sweden or places like that, it is more dangerous.' And he said: 'No, no, no. Pikes Peak is the most scary thing I have ever done.'"

Dumas says he can see Loeb's point, but he has kept going back, even after his remarkable record run, because the event has him gripped in its thrall.

LEFT: The first hill climb was run in 1916 and up until the 1990s it was a dirt track road. This photo shows a Packard taking on the Colorado mountain in 1957.

OPPOSITE: Romain Dumas's Volkswagen-sponsored record attempt from 2018.

"It was and still is completely different," Dumas says. Pikes Peak exists outside of normal international motorsport federations. The only rules, he says, are that the car has to have a complete roll cage. And the crash helmet needs to conform...

When Dumas first drove there, he says, he turned up with the helmet he had used at Le Mans. Fabricated from carbon fibre, it was the top-class helmet homologated by international governing body the FIA. Yet he was told he could not wear it because it was not approved by the Sports Car Club of America, which sanctions Pikes Peak.

The origins of this individualistic approach stretch back to the foundation of the event, by American entrepreneur Spencer Penrose, who made his money in mining and real estate and settled with his fortune in nearby Colorado Springs.

Penrose built the road up Pikes Peak and first staged a race up it in 1916. It soon grew in

popularity. For a long time, the course was gravel. From 2002, paving began, in sections, until the first all-asphalt event in 2012; coincidentally, the year Dumas first competed.

Over the years, some of the biggest names in motorsport have been drawn by the challenge. American racing legend Bobby Unser set a series of course records in the 1950s and 1960s. Loeb was not the first world rally star to conquer the course – that was Finn Ari Vatanen, another world champion, who used a Peugeot 406 Turbo 16 to break the record in 1988. Over the years, despite the switch from gravel to asphalt, Pikes Peak's essential nature has remained unchanged.

"They call it unlimited," says Dumas, who plies his trade in endurance racing most of the time. "It really means what it says. You can do whatever you want, there is no minimum weight, no maximum power. Everything is free.

"You can see any kind of cars, with completely different ideas, so it is why I loved this race when

ABOVE: Sébastien Loeb re-set the Pikes Peak hill climb record in 2013. He got to the top of the 20km run in 8 minutes and 13 seconds in his Peugeot 208 T16.

ABOVE LEFT: Romain Dumas keeps coming back for more. Here he waits on the startline in a Ford Performance SuperVan during the Pikes Peak International Hill Climb, The Race to the Clouds, in 2023.

OPPOSITE: If the drops over the edge weren't frightening enough on smooth Tarmac, drivers have to cope with a road surface that is subjected to extremes of cold on a 4,300 metre (14,000 ft) mountain.

I came with my own team. You can fight with and beat a factory effort just because you have different ideas. It is the last place in motorsport where, with a little less money, you can still achieve a lot."

"You start at 2,400 metres (7,874 ft), you end up at 4,200 metres (13,780 ft). All within in 20km (12 miles). The temperature will go from 20°C (70°F) at the start to 0°C (32°F) at the top. The air density is so low that the brakes are also fading

during the run. And they never produce the tyres to deal with this kind of stress. In 8 minutes, in 20km, you see completely different scenery. At the start, there are a lot of trees. You go over 3,500 metres (11,483 ft), the density of the air is so low that the trees disappear. And when you finish above 4,000 metres (13,123 ft), it is like being on the moon. There is nothing left any more, only stones.

"The bad point is that it is very dangerous at the speed we are going. No barriers. People complain that now it is all Tarmac, while in the past it was on gravel. But at the end of the day, with gravel you are sliding at 80km/h (50mph), with Tarmac, you are sliding at 140km/h (90mph)." He laughs, not nervously, but in a way that portrays the jeopardy of what he is describing. "So if you fly, you fly a lot longer when it's on Tarmac, you know...?"

Ah, yes. The danger. There are films of both Vatanen's and Dumas's runs, and you watch them open-mouthed. At times, the road runs right to the edge of the mountain, and the drop beyond its edge looks as if it goes on forever.

"You would fall for a long time," Dumas says. "It depends on the corner." He has never checked to see which ones have the biggest drops? "No," he says. "You don't want to look."

His record run, he says, "...was amazing – it was really fast. We did a lot of sim (work). But the car was gorgeous. We could have gone faster but on purpose we reduced the power to make sure we had no issues with the battery. But it was... Phwoar, it was something big."

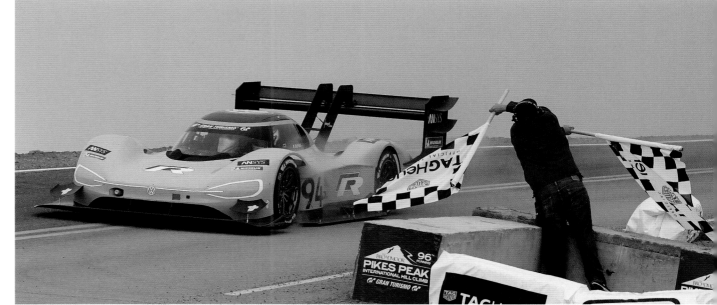

OPPOSITE: Australian Brett Dickie driving a Honda S2000 in one of the frequent barrier-less stretches of the ascent in 2023.

ABOVE RIGHT: Celebrating the first sub-eight-minute run on Pikes Peak. Unlike Sébastien Loeb, Dumas keeps going back.

RIGHT: For a Pikes Peak regular like Dumas, the chequered flags are purely symbolic. He knows where the line is.

Prescott

Gloucestershire, England

Hill climbs these days hark back to a bygone age before professionalism, when even at the highest level drivers risked their lives for minimal financial reward.

Leading circuit racing drivers make potfuls of money, but in hill climbing people still risk their lives simply for the love of the sport. Prescott just outside Cheltenham in England's famous Cotswolds is one of the places loved the most.

Until the 1960s, the leading drivers of their era competed at Prescott. Before World War II, Hans Stuck drove one of the mighty Auto Union grand prix cars there. Post-war, the likes of Stirling Moss, Jim Clark and Graham Hill cut their teeth up the scenic hill.

Hill climb events take place under the radar, but a measure of Prescott's standing is that it has twice featured on the BBC's *Top Gear* programme – in the ultra-successful era of hosts Jeremy Clarkson, Richard Hammond and James May.

Prescott was founded when the Bugatti Owners' Club was looking for a permanent home that could remove them from the constant complaints about noise they were experiencing at temporary venues. They bought the land of the Prescott estate in 1938, and created a short run up the drive of about 800 metres (2,625 ft). It was expanded to 1,031 metres (3,383 ft) in 1960. That kilometre packs a lot in.

Andy Priaulx is one of the most successful touring car drivers in history – he won the European championship in 2004 followed by the world title three times in a row from 2005–7. What is less known is that Priaulx cut his teeth in hill climbs, following in the footsteps of his father Graham, and was 1995 British champion.

Priaulx broke the Prescott hill record on his first appearance there, and he says: "There is something like an energy that lives in the track. It's a difficult one to explain, but you get it when you drive into Monza, when everyone lines up on the grid at Silverstone. All the hairs stand up. You know when you're driving you're kind of making a piece of history each time."

As at most hill climbs, there are not extensive safety features. Priaulx says: "It's super, super dangerous – it's old-school and requires quite a lot of courage. Especially driving the V8s now with all the power. The road runs away from you pretty quick in those sorts of cars. You have be on your A-game."

Hill-climbing gives drivers very limited time on track, and Priaulx says it requires a particular extemporaneous kind of skill that is less important at a circuit race.

"You're always going into that first corner and it's an act of faith," he says. "It takes some sort of intuition. You have an expectation of what you think the car can do but you're not 100% sure but you have to put it on the line anyway.

"I guess it's a bit like going into Turn 1 off the start on a circuit race on slicks on a damp, drying track. That's what hill-climbing taught me.

"If you go safe, you'll be slow. You need 100% aggression with 10% restraint and it's that ragged edge that is an intuitive, instinctive, optimistic, opportunistic kind of state of driving."

OPPOSITE: Prescott is the home of the Bugatti Owners' Club, so it's appropriate that a Bugatti Veyron should be featured, seen here exiting Pardon hairpin.

TOP: Leading on from Pardon hairpin is a fast right-left known as the Esses. Prescott hosts a wide variety of vintage and single-marque events through the year as well as rounds of the British and Midland Hill Climb Championships.

ABOVE: Finishing the 1,030 metre (3,379 ft) course is the corner known as Semi-Circle.

Rally Finland

Jyväskylä, Finland

Finland's 1,000 Lakes Rally is so difficult, so far out of the norm for most racing drivers, that it took 40 years before it was won by a driver who was not from Scandinavia. Officially known these days as Rally Finland, it is held in the country's central region, around the town of Jyväskylä. It is the fastest rally in the world championship and arguably the most demanding.

This is a region of drumlins and eskers, landscape features created when glaciers bulldozed over rock outcrops, rounding them off. They account for the strange, undulating landscape that generates a key feature of the rally – 'yumps', or jumps, in the road. The multiplicity of lakes gives the region its name, and makes the map almost as much blue as green. This is a sparsely populated region and, like so many rural areas, it is becoming more so. But the peaceful nature of the setting belies the extremes of the sensory overload of its signature event.

The smooth gravel roads of the region are flanked by pine forests and feature a multitude of high-speed corners. The 'yumps' are crests over which cars are regularly, and spectacularly,

launched into the air – sometimes even in the middle of corners.

First held in 1951, it became a world championship round in 1973. Its record holders are two Finnish legends – Hannu Mikkola with

seven wins in total and Tommi Mäkinen with five in a row. But so different is the character of the rally, so extreme the demands of precision at high speed required to set quick times and not crash, that it took until 1990 for a driver who was not from Finland or Sweden to win it. Only six

OPPOSITE: Swedish driver Oliver Solberg (son of 2003 World Champion Petter) takes a 'yump' in the 2023 Rally Finland in his Škoda Fabia RS.

RIGHT: Like ski-jumping, the distance travelled is marked out for spectators, though no marks for style. This is Takamoto Katsuta in his Toyota GR Yaris Rally1 Hybrid giving it 'big air'.

others have since repeated the feat. The man who achieved history was Spain's Carlos Sainz, then on his way to the first of his two world rally titles with Toyota. "It is such high speed that even if I tried to explain it to you, you would not understand," Sainz says. "The speed is so high that it's amazing. You have these crests in the middle of the corners where you are sliding and at the same time you are jumping sideways.

"You are talking about travelling at 160, 170, 180km/h (100–110mph), and when you sit in the car there and you finish the stage, you really feel as if you were on the edge. It is really something else and that is why it is a rally that has been dominated so many years by the Scandinavian drivers because they know the roads very well and the technique."

The 'yumps' are so central to the experience of the rally that spectators measure the distance travelled by cars in the air on the famous Ouninpohja section. The record is held by Estonian Markko Martin, who in 2003 leapt 57 metres (187 ft) at a speed of 171km/h (106mph).

For Sainz, regarded as one of the greatest rally drivers in history, his victory in 1990 was the third of his career. He went on to take 26, and has also won the Dakar Rally four times. But that win in Finland remains one of his most cherished.

"You need to concentrate only on the speed, and the line has to be perfect," Sainz says. "One of my wishes when I started in the WRC was to try to win that rally. For me to become the first non-Scandinavian to win was something very special."

OPPOSITE: Pierre-Louis Loubet of France in the Ford Puma Rally1 Hybrid applies the technique described above by Carlos Sainz through the forests of Jyväskylä.

TOP RIGHT: Red Bull-sponsored Nikolay Gryazin negotiates a bridge in the Škoda Fabia Rally2 Evo.

RIGHT: Finnish driver Teemu Suninen executes a sideways 'yump' in his Hyundai i20 N Rally1 Hybrid.

Red Bull Ring

Spielberg, Austria

The Österreichring, the forerunner of the Red Bull Ring which hosts the modern Austrian Grand Prix, was one of the world's great circuits. A 5.94km (3.69 mile), high-speed blast through the foothills of the Styrian Alps, past some of the loveliest scenery at any race circuit anywhere, it was a test for the drivers like few others have ever been.

"It was a mighty track," says John Watson, who won there in 1976. "It was quick corners, the middle part of the circuit is really the only bit left now that's realistic to when I raced there. And then you had the Bosch Kurve at the end of the long back straight. A semi-banked corner, long, long, long corner. It was just a lovely race track to drive."

Ah, the Bosch Kurve. Every corner at the old Österreichring was fast and long, but only some have gone down in legend. Another was the final corner, the Rindt Kurve, another high-speed, right-hander.

"It was a bit bumpy mid to exit of the corner," says Watson, "but once you had made your apex, it was all about releasing the car to the very edge of the race track, trying to mitigate any slip angle – or what you might call in old-school terms the drift – so when you exited the corner you were definitely pointing in a straight line and maintaining as good an exit

speed as possible, not inhibited by too much sideways or scrubbing."

But the Bosch Kurve was even better.

Approached down a long, curving straight where Formula 1 cars topped 200mph (320km/h), the Bosch Kurve was a gear or two down, banked, with a grandstand on the outside right up against the track. "Daunting," says Watson. "You are coming at it from very high speed. There was no run-off. The barrier about six feet back from the edge of the race track, and behind that a grandstand."

His victory, the only one achieved by the short-lived F1 team owned by American racing mogul Roger Penske, came on the one-year anniversary of the death of their talisman, Mark Donohue, a close friend of Penske.

OPPOSITE: Didier Pironi (Ferrari) leads Nigel Mansell (Lotus), John Watson (McLaren) and Riccardo Patrese (Arrows) through the Hella Licht chicane in the 1981 race.

TOP: Looking past Ronnie Peterson's JPS Lotus in 1978 towards the top of the hill where today the circuit takes a sharp right.

MIDDLE: Vittorio Brambilla on his way to a popular – and unexpected – win in Austria..

BOTTOM: Andrea de Cesaris extricates himself from his Ligier after a spectacular accident in the 1985 Austrian Grand Prix.

Donohue died when he suffered a brain hemorrhage after a crash at the circuit's first corner – another fast right-hander called Hella Licht, which was slowed down with a chicane two years later.

The grand prix at which Donohue lost his life has entered racing legend because the winner crashed right after taking the flag. Held in torrential rain, it was won by Italian Vittorio Brambilla, who had a reputation for wildness and whose nickname was 'The Monza Gorilla' for his rough-and-ready approach to racing.

Somehow, that day, at one of the world's most challenging circuits, in the most difficult possible conditions, Brambilla failed to live up to his nickname – at least until he started waving frantically in delight after he had crossed the finish line. Not quite believing what he had just achieved, the extent of his celebrations causing him to lose control of his March car and crunch its orange nose cone into the barrier.

Perhaps the most dramatic race on the old Österreichring, though, was in 1982. It should

have been dominated by the turbo cars that by now were taking a stranglehold on F1, their power finally mated to decent chassis and beginning to call time on the venerable old Cosworth DFV V8 which had ruled the roost since 1967, bar Ferrari's flat-12 era of the mid-to-late 1970s.

One by one the turbos failed, and when Alain Prost's Renault, the last one standing, retired from the lead with a handful of laps to go, victory was disputed by the Lotus of Elio de Angelis and Williams's Keke Rosberg, neither of whom had won a grand prix before.

De Angelis had been ahead throughout, but Rosberg began to close in rapidly, at a rate of around 1.5 seconds a lap, and they entered the final lap with the Italian just 1.6 seconds ahead. At the last corner, De Angelis slid wide on the exit and Rosberg got a run on him. They crossed the line side by side, the Lotus ahead by just 0.05 seconds.

The track held the Austrian GP for another five years, amid increasing concern about safety caused by its narrowness and high speeds.

A massive barrel-roll by Andrea de Cesaris's Ligier at the Texaco chicane in 1985 was a warning sign. But the 1987 race proved a turning point.

In practice, Stefan Johansson's McLaren hit a deer, the driver lucky not to be injured, and Nelson Piquet's Williams set pole at an average of 256.621km/h (159.457mph). The race had to be started three times following two multiple pile-ups on the narrow start-finish straight. After that, the track was deemed too fast and dangerous, and fell off the calendar for 10 years.

OPPOSITE: An aerial view of the Red Bull Ring shows the wooded ridge to the left separating the old Österreichring track from the modern circuit. The Bosch Kurve grandstand is visible below the cloud with the old track passing directly in front.

BELOW LEFT: Mick Schumacher (Haas) and Antonio Giovinazzi (Alfa Romeo) go side by side in Turn 3 at the 2021 Styrian Grand Prix.

BELOW: Max Verstappen lost it in the final corner during practice in 2019 but went on to win the race, Honda's first since their return to Formula 1 in 2015.

In the mid-1990s, the circuit was totally rebuilt by Franz Wurz, a leading rallycross driver in the 1970s and the father of Alex Wurz, who was beginning to make his way in a racing career that was to lead him to F1, two Le Mans wins and his position as chairman of the Grand Prix Drivers' Association. The civil engineer on the project was Hermann Tilke, in his first foray into race-track building, starting out on the route that led him to become F1's go-to architect.

Many have bemoaned the loss of a classic track, but the old Österreichring layout had to be shortened. There was no run-off at the Bosch and Rindt Kurves and the land all around was owned by local residents.

"This is why we had to place the current Turn 3 at the exact distance to those homes," says Alex Wurz, "and the hill behind the grandstands between Turns 1 and 3 works as a noise barrier. The issue was always that the grounds all around belonged to the farmers, so it was complex to get everyone to approve it. That's what my dad did – to negotiate with more than 20 landowners and all the (local) governments. This was the time when run-offs got larger and larger and most of the corners were designed by the centimetre to fit the property boundaries."

So while the new track resembled the old in terms of shape, its length was now 4.31km (2.68 miles) and all the great corners had gone in the name of safety. The new circuit had nothing like the challenge of the old track, but its second half, starting with the two quick left-handers at Turns 6 and 7 and leading to the fast and challenging final two corners, has proved itself since its debut in 1997 as a place that generates great racing.

TOP LEFT: Charles Leclerc approaches Turn 9, the Rindt Kurve, a part of the track common to both old and new circuits.

LEFT: The kerbing on the outside of Turn 1, the Niki Lauda Kurve, bears the marks of regular first lap battles.

It fell off the F1 calendar again in 2003, a year after one of the most controversial finishes in history. Rubens Barrichello, who had dominated the race, was ordered to hand victory to his Ferrari teammate Michael Schumacher, even though the German was already completely dominating the season and his championship was under no threat. The pair were booed on the podium, and Schumacher rather sheepishly pulled Barrichello up onto the top step with him. It did little to quieten the opprobrium and generated a $1m fine for Ferrari from the FIA for compromising the podium ceremony.

In 2006, Red Bull co-owner Dietrich Mateschitz bought the track and renovated it, as part of a campaign to regenerate the local region, and in 2014, it returned to the F1 schedule, money for the hosting fee no longer an issue. A pale shadow of its former glory, but a fun little track nonetheless.

ABOVE: Max Verstappen leads through Turn 3 in front of his regular 'Oranj Army' who pack out the stands at the Red Bull Ring each year.

RIGHT: Verstappen heads into Turn 4, now at a far greater distance from the old Bosch Kurve grandstand.

Road America

Elkhart Lake, Wisconsin, USA

Road America near Elkhart Lake in Wisconsin is not only one of the greatest race tracks in the USA, it is also one of the few in the world still using its original layout.

They very much got it right first time when they built a circuit in farm country, half way between Milwaukee and Green Bay, two and a half hours north of Chicago, in 1955. So right, in fact, that it was entered in the national register of historic places in 2006.

If there is anything that goes against Road America, it's the location. As McLaren Racing's chief executive officer Zak Brown says: "Awesome circuit but it's kind of in the middle of nowhere."

But ask drivers about the 6.51km (4.04 mile) layout and the words they will use most commonly are "flowing" and "challenging". Its best corner is known as 'The Kink', Turn 11, which comes after a tricky double right-hander known as Carousel.

F1 driver Kevin Magnussen, who has driven an IndyCar and a sports prototype at Road America, says The Kink is "super on the limit". Two-time IndyCar champion Gil de Ferran said: "Sometimes you had to set up the car to be a little bit on the nose so it doesn't understeer too much everywhere else, and that kink can be very hairy."

The Kink puts drivers in an almost impossible quandary, Magnussen says, between whether to take it flat out, or not quite. "It's really on the edge," Magnussen says. "There is an upshift right before you go in. If you lift, you shouldn't have upshifted. And if you don't upshift then you are in the limiter."

Road America – sometimes also known after the nearby town Elkhart Lake which put on street races in 1951/2 – hosts IndyCars, endurance racing, TransAm and bikes. It hosted its first IndyCar race in 1982, fell off the calendar in 2006 after the reunification of the rival Indy Racing League and Champ Car series, and returned for good in 2016.

The list of winners is like a *Who's Who* of the big names of IndyCar over the past 40 years – Mario Andretti and his son Michael have each won it three times, Emerson Fittipaldi, Jacques Villeneuve, Scott Dixon, Josef Newgarden and Alex Palou twice – underlining its status as one of America's prime driving challenges.

And like all challenging tracks, it can bite – and not just from the difficulty of the layout. Brazilian Cristiano da Matta hit a deer in an IndyCar test in 2006, suffering a subdural hematoma. He recovered, and did return to racing, but his career at the top level was effectively finished.

Even without the challenge posed by unsuspecting local wildlife, the track puts drivers through the mill. Magnussen says the whole circuit, which is made up of straights, big braking points, and lots of medium-speed corners, is extremely tough.

"In an IndyCar there's no power steering and in the high-speed corners the steering wheel becomes super heavy and it's bumpy and stiff. Driving one at Road America is one of the most physical things you can do in a race car."

OPPOSITE: The first lap of the 2023 Sonsio Grand Prix. Road America bears certain similarities to England's Oulton Park, set in 640 acres (250 hectares) of parkland with many elevation changes.

BELOW: The 2023 Indy 500 winner, Josef Newgarden during practice for the Sonsio Grand Prix held at Road America.

Saint-Gouéno

Saint-Gouéno, Brittany, France

On the map, the rural D14 between Collinée and Saint-Gouéno in Brittany looks like so many other roads, winding through the rural countryside of one of the highest areas of the Côtes D'Armor. Chance upon it in a car without knowing its history and it seems like the local authorities have been ultra-cautious with their road safety, placing double Armco barriers at almost all of the bends. Some of them don't seem that precipitous either. When the succession of barriers continues for 3.2km (2 miles), that's when the penny drops. This is a road used for motorsport.

Two other tiny clues to its annual use as a hillclimb course are thin white lines drawn across the Tarmac by the Départ et les Hautières and the Arrivée et Haut de l'Hiver.

The Saint-Gouéno hillclimb celebrated its 38th running in 2023 and is part of the Championnat de France de la Montagne. Along with the French championship, which draws entries from as far away as Chamrousse near Grenoble, there is the British and Irish contingent competing in the Hillclimb Masters, a trio of three events of which the Breton dash is the finale.

Though many motorsport venues are in the countryside, Saint-Gouéno is perhaps the most bucolic location of all. Travel the route during the week, and you're likely to meet a farm vehicle somewhere on the course.

Unlike Goodwood, where there is a paddock at the top of the hill which collects the cars before a return run down the hill, Saint-Gouéno has a rural loop taking cars past farms and fields and at one point through a small hamlet.

Cars assemble in the *pre-grille* area, a lane outside the paddock, and are then led in a convoy of about 15–20 vehicles through the twisty lanes, hamlets and farmyards to the startline. Once their run is completed, there is a short return on a single-track road to the paddock. All this supervised by the ACO, Automobile Club de l'Ouest, organisers of Le Mans.

For hill climb aficionados it's described as 'a bit like Wiscombe park in Devon only much longer and much faster'. John Lloyd, a British ex-pat living in Côtes d'Armor, has been organising the British and Irish side of things for 12 years and welcomes back familiar faces each time.

OPPOSITE: Irish driver Ben O'Brien tackles the *fer a cheval* (horseshoe) to post the fastest time of the British and Irish Masters field – a 1:30.474 in his Gould GR37-Judd.

TOP: En route to the starting line through the lanes and farmyards of Brittany.

ABOVE RIGHT AND RIGHT: Cars form up in the lane the *pre-grille* area to be taken in convoy to the start line 2km (1.2 miles) away.

Silverstone

Northamptonshire, England

Lewis Hamilton has a special connection with Silverstone. At the time of writing, he has won here eight times, equalling the record for wins at a track. He shares it with himself, in Hungary, and Michael Schumacher at the French Grand Prix.

Silverstone is also the place where Hamilton scored what arguably remains his greatest ever victory, a virtuoso performance in the rain in 2008 where he beat the second-placed car by over a minute and lapped everyone up to third place.

At times that day, Hamilton was circulating Silverstone 5 seconds (and more) faster than any other driver. Conditions were so bad that Felipe Massa, Hamilton's title rival in 2008, spun no less than five times. It was a drive to compare with Schumacher's famous win in Spain in 1996, or Ayrton Senna's in Portugal in 1985. Or, indeed, Senna's win at Silverstone 20 years before Hamilton, in 1988.

Silverstone — wet or dry — is the kind of circuit that sorts the great from the merely good. But in the wet, it is a special challenge. The land here on the Northamptonshire plateau is so flat it feels as if you can see the curvature of the earth. It is brutally exposed to the wind, which often seems to make Silverstone several degrees colder than elsewhere in this part of England, and that wind plays havoc with the aerodynamics of an F1 car.

Mark Webber, British Grand Prix winner for Red Bull in 2010 and 2012, used to say he would judge the wind direction from the flags on the British Racing Drivers' Clubhouse roof before starting his qualifying lap, to understand in which way the car would behave in certain corners.

Combine this with Silverstone's predominance of high-speed corners, and you have a circuit drivers revere and adore. Throw in rain as well, and the combination of a slippery surface with some of the fastest and most demanding corners on the F1 calendar, and you have a recipe for the truly special drivers to stand out, through a combination of ability and confidence.

It takes a special talent to commit hard to corners such as Copse and the Becketts complex when the rain is pouring down and grip levels are changing from lap to lap. To have the confidence that your talent won't let you down opens the door for it to shine, while other, less gifted, drivers will be cautious, concerned about what could go wrong.

Hamilton lapped his McLaren teammate Heikki Kovalainen that day in 2008, and the team's test driver at the time, Pedro de la Rosa, explains why.

"It's a combination of everything," the Spaniard says, "but it's mostly down to talent, obviously, and his real strength came when no-one could put the tyre into the operating window because there was too much water, the intermediates were not working. That's what happened in Silverstone in that race. It's because of his way of sliding the car into the corner — he's drifting. He's not fighting the car.

"If you look at Lewis's onboard camera, you would say he is massively smooth. He doesn't turn the wheel much. But the car is on the knife-edge, although you don't appreciate that on the on-board camera. And being on a knife-edge means it is drifting, sliding, and it is generating tyre temperature, and that's how he drives. No matter what type of corner, in which conditions, he will always go to the knife-edge on the entry phase.

OPPOSITE: Lewis Hamilton celebrates after his victory against the odds in 2021. After his bitter title battle with Max Verstappen finally reached boiling point in a collision at Copse on the first lap, the Mercedes driver fought back from a penalty and chased down Ferrari's Charles Leclerc to extend his record of home wins to eight.

BELOW: Hamilton put in a performance worthy of the title he was to win that year by dominating in the wet at Silverstone in 2008.

"The difference with Heikki Kovalainen, for example, was massive because of that. Heikki was not able to generate the temperature needed during a race. He lost the temperature, he was becoming slower and slower and Lewis was just quicker and quicker and quicker."

Hamilton's victory that day was a fitting way to mark the 50th anniversary of the self-styled home of British motorsport.

Silverstone arose out of a World War II bomber training base. In 1948, the Royal Automobile Club under chairman Wilfred Andrews was casting around for a site to host a grand prix and in August arranged a lease with the Royal Air Force and employed a man called James Brown to create the circuit in less than two months. Brown – who remained employed by the circuit until his death nearly 40 years later – hit gold first time.

The familiar layout, adopted from 1950 until 1975, had just eight corners, but what corners they were. With names such as Copse, Maggotts, Chapel, Becketts, Stowe, Club, Abbey and Woodcote, they have become embedded in motorsport lore.

In the years before aerodynamic downforce, it was Woodcote, the final bend, that was the classic; a long, fast right-hander which became famous as the place to watch the likes of Jochen Rindt and Ronnie Peterson, car-control masters, in a high-speed four-wheel drift.

Jim Clark was the master of this layout, with five victories in six years through the 1960s. But perhaps the most famous race was in 1969, when Rindt in his Lotus fought a duel with Jackie Stewart in his Matra, leaving the rest far behind. Lap after lap they circulated in tandem, these two great friends and rivals, slipstreaming, swapping places, occasionally looking across at each other and smiling as they hurtled side by side down the straights. That was until a loose rear wing, that was rubbing on a rear tyre, eventually brought Rindt into the pits.

The death knell was sounded for the original track in 1973, when Jody Scheckter lost control of his McLaren at Woodcote and triggered an 11-car pile-up that blocked the pit straight and caused the race to be stopped. Amazingly, given the fragility of the cars of the day and their tendency to catch fire, no one was hurt.

The crash, though, crystallised a feeling that Woodcote had become simply too fast as the cars' speeds had increased, and for the next

ABOVE LEFT: A landmark event, the 1951 British Grand Prix marked the first win for Ferrari with Argentine driver José Froilán González (12) taking victory from Fangio's Alfa Romeo.

ABOVE: Jackie Stewart turns in to Copse corner in the 1973 race.

OPPOSITE TOP: A good view of the old pit lane at Silverstone from 1979 with the Ferraris of Gilles Villeneuve (12) and Jody Sheckter (11).

OPPOSITE LEFT: John Watson leads McLaren teammate Andrea de Cesaris in 1981.

OPPOSITE RIGHT: Buoyed by the crowd, Nigel Mansell's 1987 victory was one of the greatest pursuits in F1 history.

British Grand Prix at Silverstone, in 1975, a chicane was inserted.

Silverstone might now be considered the immutable home of the UK's F1 world championship race, but for a long time it alternated as host, first with Aintree from 1955 until 1962, and then from 1964 until 1986 with Brands Hatch in Kent . While Silverstone is flat and featureless, Brands had the benefit of topography – located partly in a natural amphitheatre, with

significant undulations that featured in classic corners such as Paddock Hill Bend, before heading out into the woods for high-speed corners such as Hawthorns and Westfield.

But in the 1980s, when motorsport's authorities instigated a policy of long-term contracts with single circuits for grands prix, Silverstone got the nod. It was perceived not only as the more up-to-date facility, but one that also had more room to expand and modernize, and it won the deal.

The 1985 race was the last held on the layout with the Woodcote chicane, and it marked a significant landmark in F1 history. Keke Rosberg took pole position in his Williams-Honda FW10 with the first ever lap with an average in excess of 260km/h (160mph), and he did it with a slow puncture that caused the Finn a lurid moment as he fought his sliding car through the chicane towards the finish line. The crowd in the grandstand, who numbered this writer among them, gasped in admiration – and then

cheered when the time was announced – 1:05.591 seconds, 258.984km/h (160.925mph). As well as a historic landmark, it was also a stark illustration of the rate of progress in F1. Two years previously, René Arnoux had set pole for Ferrari with an equally spectacular lap... which took 1:09.462.

There were other milestone moments at Silverstone, too. In 1977, Renault gave their turbo car its first outing. In 1981, John Watson's McLaren took the first victory for a car whose chassis was made of carbon-fibre. In 1987, the circuit celebrated its new contract with a revised layout – and one of the greatest races in its history. The Woodcote chicane was removed and the cars slowed before the corner with a new chicane on the straight just before it.

It was a year of Williams-Honda domination, and Nigel Mansell sent the home fans into raptures with one of his best drives. Changing strategy to make a mid-race stop for tyres, he rejoined 29 seconds behind teammate Nelson Piquet with 28 laps remaining, and chased the Brazilian down, overtaking him with a superlative 'dummy' pass into Stowe with three laps to go.

On this new layout, the 'best corner' honour now fell to Club, on the Buckinghamshire side of a track that straddles two counties. Super-fast, with a downhill entry, and limited run-off, Club was a place where only the very brave tested their limits. But this new design lasted only four years before a major revamp in 1991. Now, peak Silverstone was the new Becketts complex.

OPPOSITE: The sequence of corners after the Wellington Straight – Brooklands and Luffield – allows for some unremitting wheel-to-wheel action as demonstrated by Verstappen and Leclerc in 2019.

TOP LEFT: A deserted BRDC (British Racing Drivers' Club) clubhouse for the race in 2020 celebrating Silverstone's 70 years.

LEFT: A relieved crowd at Copse Corner sees Max Verstappen walk away from his 2021 impact with the barriers.

Before, Becketts had been a relatively innocuous, medium-speed right-hander constantly in the shadow of its more demanding cousins. Now, it was turned into a high-speed series of five S-bends, opening out onto Hangar Straight, while Club was neutered with a chicane before it. Towards the end of the lap, too, big changes were made, with a new complex of corners in front of the clubhouse of owners the British Racing Drivers' Club (BRDC). This started with another fast and intimidating corner, Bridge, entered at massively high speed after the long blast from the new Club corner through the flat-out kink at Abbey.

It was on this circuit layout that Mansell mania reached its peak with the home fans. In 1990,

Mansell played to the crowd, as he often did, throwing his gloves and balaclava to the fans after his Ferrari broke down mid-race and, unhappy with the way things were going against teammate Alain Prost, announcing his retirement. Inevitably, he went back on his decision and signed for a return to Williams, and in 1991 and 1992, 140,000 fans crowded into Silverstone to watch Mansell dominate with the FW14 and then the iconic FW14B, in which he was strolling to a long-overdue world title.

Following the death of Ayrton Senna in 1994, a chicane was inserted at Abbey, to slow cars down before Bridge. But the layout remained until 2010, when it was changed yet again.

Now, Abbey was turned back into a high-speed kink, but this time to the right, leading the cars to a new 'stadium section' aimed at promoting overtaking, with two slow corners, a right and then a left, bringing the cars back out on to the old back straight of the national circuit and into the BRDC complex again.

This new design was instigated under the BRDC presidency of Damon Hill. The idea was to promote racing, but before cars had even been sent out on it Hill wondered aloud whether they had ruined the track, describing it as "a frustrating compromise" that risked "destroying the essence" of Silverstone.

Hill, who won at Silverstone in 1994 after rival Schumacher was controversially black-flagged, need not have worried. In terms of combining a challenge for the drivers with a layout that promotes racing, the new Silverstone is arguably the best track on the entire F1 calendar.

Copse, eased slightly in 1991, is now one of the most dramatic corners of the season, Becketts remains sublime, and Abbey – also flat-out in top gear in a modern F1 car in ideal conditions – can be added to the list of awe-inspiring high-speed corners. And there is something about the combination of corners through the new stadium section and down to Brooklands, and then out of Becketts through Stowe and down to the chicane at Vale-Club that promotes thrilling racing.

In 2019, Charles Leclerc and Max Verstappen staged a man-to-man duel for the best part of half the race that will go down as one of the greatest pieces of wheel-to-wheel competition the sport has ever seen, and which drew comparisons with the famous scrap between Gilles Villeneuve and René Arnoux at the 1979 French Grand Prix.

In 2021, Fernando Alonso used all his guile and racing intelligence to pass six cars on the first

lap of the sprint race at Silverstone and move up from 11th to fifth in his Alpine. And in 2022, Leclerc was at it again. Hung out to dry in the lead by Ferrari after choosing not to stop him for fresh tyres under a late safety car, while all the cars behind him did, Leclerc fought like a lion in defence, even passing Hamilton around the outside of Copse on his worn tyres at one point, even if in the end it was in vain.

And perhaps the most striking example was in 2021, when Hamilton and Max Verstappen staged a first half-lap of incredible intensity as their championship duel came to a head before finally colliding at Copse. Few tracks would enable racing of such fierceness. But few have been guided through the decades with such wisdom and care. "Silverstone is just a great layout," Hamilton says. "One of the best tracks to drive."

OPPOSITE TOP: After years of wrangling with FIA chief Max Mosley and F1 rights-holder Bernie Ecclestone, Silverstone finally got the investment to build a world-class facility.

OPPOSITE BOTTOM: Cars are rolled the final few yards onto the grid in 2022.

ABOVE: Zhou Guanyu's Alfa Romeo is pitched into an interminable slide on its roll hoop in 2022. Zhou was unhurt in the crash, which, like all accidents in F1, allow the FIA's technical team to assess the strength of safety measures.

Suzuka

Suzuka, Mie Prefecture, Japan

There is a wall on the outside of Turn 4 at Suzuka, home of the Japanese Grand Prix, that gives about as good a view as there is at a race track.

To the right, a few miles distant, the waters of Ise Bay, shimmering if it's sunny, glowering if, as can often be the case, rain is threatening or falling. A few hundred metres in front, and slightly to the left, beyond the pit straight, the big wheel of the Circuitland amusement park. Behind you, a grandstand, and behind it – unseen unless you move a little further around the track – the mountains of the Suzuka Quasi-National Park.

And in front, the most difficult section of the most demanding grand prix track in the world, the left-right-left-right-left sequence of the Esses, a swerving, undulating rollercoaster ride that every racing driver who has experienced it adores.

Fernando Alonso, who won at Suzuka in 2006 and the year before performed one of the most breathtaking passing moves at the track's daunting, flat-out 130R corner, sums it up. "Every lap is pure joy in Suzuka," he says.

"The nature of the track. The high-speed content. The first sector. Really, this kind of car comes alive thanks to the downforce and the grip we have.

"And the fans as well. Even if you don't feel them when you are driving, you feel the atmosphere of the weekend is different here, about how

enthusiastic they are and how they live the whole weekend. It is a special race, this one."

The Japanese Grand Prix at Suzuka is an all-round sensory experience. The sight of F1 cars on this uniquely demanding track is something to behold, and the atmosphere created by the highly enthusiastic local fans – who show their devotion to the sport with costumes and home-made models of Formula 1 cars worn as hats and clothing – is warmly charming.

The lap starts with a downhill pit straight that leads into a very fast right-hander, on the exit of which drivers have to turn and brake down into the slower Turn 2, where the track starts to go uphill again. A short straight to the sometimes flat-out kink of Turn 3 and the start of the Esses. Uphill through the right of 4 and left of 5, the driver balancing brakes and throttle and steering to measure the change of direction just so. The hill crests on the turn-in to 6 and then plunges down before rising uphill again through the fast left of Turn 7, also known as Dunlop, where Jules Bianchi was killed in the damp and gloom of 2014, his head smashing into a tractor which was recovering another car.

RIGHT: There is an innocent joyfulness about the Japanese fans at Suzuka, who treat their favourite teams and drivers with a reverence unlike elsewhere else.

OPPOSITE: The 2023 grid about to start the parade lap. The slightly downhill start at Suzuka can occasionally catch drivers out.

Dunlop marks the end of the first sector, which most drivers will say is the most challenging piece of track on the calendar.

Ferrari's Charles Leclerc says: "All the drivers — we love the first sector. It's such an incredible challenge, such a high-speed section and also corner after corner. If you miss one, then you miss the whole section. That's what makes it so exciting, driving-wise."

If the first sector was the only good bit of Suzuka, it would still be a classic track. But it's far from it, the challenges just keep coming.

Uphill through and out of Dunlop, the track begins to flatten out as round and round it goes to the left. A short straight brings the drivers past 'spider alley', a pathway squeezing through the barriers that separate this section of track from the run-off at 130R, the flat-out third-last corner, on the unique figure-of-eight layout.

But the drivers are not thinking about giant arachnids suspended from catch fencing, they're judging the entry to the Degners, perhaps the most precarious section of the track.

Degner One is a fast flick to the right, after a bare dab on the brakes, but the exit leads straight into the braking zone for the much tighter Degner Two, where the exit is narrow, and it's all too easy to slide out onto the kerb. Do that, and likely as not, you will be sucked into the barriers, so close to the track.

OPPOSITE: The infamous flashpoint from 1989 when Alain Prost turned in on teammate Ayrton Senna at the final chicane.

ABOVE LEFT: In 2002, Allan McNish was able to walk away from a monster crash in his Toyota at the flat-out 130R.

LEFT: Suzuka is the only current figure-of-eight circuit with the crossover point coming after Degner Two (lower) and the approach to 130R (higher).

Make it through Degner Two and there is a straight and then a right-hand kink which forms the braking zone for the hairpin, which exits uphill on to the long, slow, right-bending 'straight' towards Spoon Curve, a tricky double left-hander.

Falling, falling all the way through Spoon, wide on to the kerb on the exit and then the track climbs again, all the way up to 130R.

Once flat-out (reserved only for the bravest), it was opened out a little after Allan McNish had a huge accident there in a Toyota in the 2002 grand prix. It was here that Alonso went around the outside of Michael Schumacher as he climbed up through the field in 2005, the Renault's apex speed 333km/h (207mph) as the Spaniard blasted past the Ferrari, daring Schumacher to try to fight.

Through 130R and a short straight to the only clumsy corner on the track, the chicane where Ayrton Senna and Alain Prost infamously collided in 1989 at the peak of their bitter rivalry. But there's still the last corner to go. It's a flat-out downhill right-hander that looks as if it should be easy, but is far from it – the car under load, the track falling away, it's all too easy to misjudge it and run too wide. Do that and a massive accident awaits, as Timo Glock discovered in 2008, Robert Kubica in 2019 and Logan Sargeant in 2023.

The track is made more special for the drivers because it is what is known as 'old school'. That means mistakes are punished. The walls are close, there are things to hit, so there is real jeopardy around a layout that already tests their skills to the limit.

As Max Verstappen puts it: "There are a few tracks that have sectors that are very quick, like in Austin. But what makes Suzuka very special is that there is no run-off, so if you have a moment, you're going off. In Austin, you have

the run-off and Tarmac and normally it's a bit more forgiving. So that's why this track is really beautiful to drive once the car is planted."

Who designed this magic 5.81km (3.60 miles) of asphalt, perhaps unsurpassed anywhere in the world? The popular answer is venerated Dutch track architect John Hugenholtz, who also designed elements of the Zandvoort track. But the truth is not quite so clear-cut.

The track was the idea of Soichiro Honda, founder of the eponymous car company. Honda wanted a test and race track, and he wanted it to be good. The first idea was to demolish a rice farm, but Honda forbade that, saying the company could not possibly tear down a place that created a food so intrinsic to the culture of Japan.

The site where Suzuka now sits, about an hour or so's drive south-west of Nagoya, was a piece of hill forest no one happened to be using, conveniently located not far from Honda's factory. The track makes use of its contours so beautifully, so organically, that it appears to be built, not so much on the landscape but a part of it.

Honda's archive documents the gestation of the track, and it proves that the basic shape, including its figure-of-eight layout, was laid out before Hugenholtz was employed as a design consultant. His version tidies up what was originally a longer first sector that wound around itself with predominantly slow corners, and laid the foundation for the Esses. But there were two iterations further before the final layout, a combined effort of Hugenholtz and Honda's own engineers, was settled upon.

The track opened in September 1962 and the first race held was for motor bikes. The following year, the amusement park next door, the idea of Honda's business partner Takeo Fujisawa, was opened. The vision of Fujisawa, who had a marketing bent to Honda's engineering one, was that Honda built cars and motorcycles, Suzuka was a place to watch them, but the company was also obligated to attract the next generations to racing. Fujisawa wanted Japan's children to have fun with cars, and mini-cars for kids on a mini-racetrack are among the attractions at Circuitland.

Suzuka was soon part of the fabric of Japanese racing, but it took 25 years before it hosted its

first grand prix, and was beaten to that honour by Fuji, which is owned by Honda's arch rival Toyota. Fuji Speedway (see page 109) hosted the famous 1976 title showdown between James Hunt and Niki Lauda, and another race in 1977, when debris from an accident involving Gilles Villeneuve's Ferrari and Ronnie Peterson's Tyrrell killed a marshal and a photographer in a restricted area.

Japan fell off the calendar again after that, but as F1's popularity grew in the country through the 1980s, and Honda became the dominant force on track by supplying engines to the Williams

team, the company decided it wanted a race at its home track.

As soon as Suzuka made its F1 debut, it generated drama. At its inaugural race in 1987, Nigel Mansell crashed his Williams in the Esses in qualifying and was forced to miss the race through injury, handing the championship to his hated teammate Nelson Piquet.

In 1988, Ayrton Senna recovered from almost stalling at the start and dropping to 14th on the first lap to carve back through the field in drizzling rain to take the lead from McLaren

teammate Alain Prost and clinch his first world title.

A year later, their title fight ended in controversy when Prost turned in on Senna as the Brazilian tried to pass at the chicane. Prost retired, Senna continued, and recovered from a pit stop to replace a damaged front wing to win — only to be controversially disqualified for cutting the chicane, handing the title to Prost.

That decision, which Senna blamed on FIA president Jean-Marie Balestre, led directly to another controversy in 1990. Senna, angered when Balestre refused his request to move pole onto the racing line, where there was more grip, decided that if Prost, now at Ferrari, beat him away from the line, the Frenchman would get no further than the first corner. Senna was true to his word, smashing into the back of Prost at the first corner and taking both out, ensuring he won the title.

In 1994, Damon Hill drove the race of his life in awful conditions to beat Michael Schumacher on aggregate timings after a mid-race red flag and take the title fight to the final race in Australia. Six years later, Schumacher finally ended Ferrari's 21-year title drought with his first for the Italian team after a race-long fight with McLaren's Mika Häkkinen — opening the floodgates for five years of Ferrari domination.

And in 2005 came perhaps the best Japanese Grand Prix ever, one of the greatest races of all time. The front-runners started at the back because rain hit midway through qualifying, which was run to a single-lap format that year.

Alonso might well have won from 16th on the grid, but he was delayed by having to let Christian Klien's Red Bull back past him — despite already being 7 seconds up the road at the time — having been adjudged to have passed it illegally.

That gave a chance to Räikkönen, who started one place behind Alonso in his McLaren and also charged back up through the field. He passed the leading Renault of Giancarlo Fisichella, who started third after qualifying before the rain fell, around the outside into the first corner at the start of the last lap to take the win.

Since then, two drivers have won at Suzuka more than anyone else: Lewis Hamilton and Sebastian Vettel with four victories each. Vettel made no secret of the fact that it was his favourite circuit. Hamilton would include Silverstone, Monaco, Canada and Hungary as competition, but even he once described it as "the best week of the year".

"All medium- and high-speed corners, if you go over the white line it's grass and gravel," Hamilton says. "In many scenarios you can't even see the circuit because you're going up into the sky. The overlapping (of the track) and then the history. They don't make circuits like this any more."

OPPOSITE: The challenging sweeps of the Suzuka Esses.

ABOVE: Nico Rosberg heads towards the Degner corners in his Mercedes in 2014 with the big wheel in the Suzuka amusement park behind him.

Targa Florio

Cerda, Sicily

Helmut Marko has raced on the Nürburgring Nordschleife and the old Spa-Francorchamps, but he says the craziest, most dangerous thing he ever did was take part in the Targa Florio. In the late 1960s and early 1970s, the Austrian, famous now as Red Bull's ruthless motorsport adviser, was a world-class driver who made his name in F1 and sportscar racing.

A few weeks before his career was ended by a stone that pierced his visor during the 1972 French Grand Prix and cost him his left eye, Marko produced perhaps his greatest achievement, even for a man who won Le Mans 24 Hours twice, the second time in the famous Porsche 917.

He set the lap record at the Targa Florio in the penultimate year before the event was removed from the World Sportscar Championship because it was too dangerous. To do so, Marko made up more than two minutes on the leading Ferrari 312PB of Arturo Merzario and lost the race only when he was passed by the faster rival car on the final straight.

But when Marko arrived in Sicily to prepare in the weeks leading up to the race, he wasn't sure he even wanted to take part.

"There were talks at the time that we shouldn't race at the Nürburgring," he recalls. "But here there were donkeys with a cart in the middle of

the track, Fiat 500s, and of course no guardrails. In the villages, from the front door of houses you are jumping directly in the road."

Marko would be driving an Alfa Romeo T33/3 sports prototype. For the reconnaissance days – completed on fully open public roads – he had a car which competed in the European saloon car championship.

The lap was 72km (45 miles) long, and contained something like 900 corners. It started close to the coast in the town of Cerda, and headed up into the mountains of the Madonie Natural Park, with distant views of Mount Etna far to the east, before descending back to the sea, finishing with a 15km (9 mile) straight between Campofelice and Buonfornello.

After his first lap, Marko sought out the Alfa Romeo team boss, the legendary Carlo Chiti. "I went to Chiti and said: 'You can't be serious that we should race here with a car as fast as a Formula 1.' I was a little bit cautious, and then I thought: 'Don't be a chicken. That's how racing is.'

"With a sportscar, in fifth or fourth gear there was wheelspin because it was so slippery. And the bumps...

OPPOSITE: The Mille Miglia may have been cancelled but the Targa Florio continued in 1958. Outside the pit buildings in Cerda Luigi Musso gets into the Ferrari 250TR/58 he shared with Olivier Gendebien.

LEFT: A car crosses the *traguardo* or finish line in the 1921 event. The Targa Florio had already been running since 1906.

"I was just sliding all the time. In some areas, you could fall 300–400 metres (980–1,312 ft) if you went off. Over 72km (47 miles) there were maybe fewer flag marshals than at Silverstone for the British Grand Prix nowadays. If you did not come by, no one would miss you. It was something completely out of the racing I had seen before – an anachronism, even then."

Marko's point about no one knowing if something had gone wrong had been proven right the previous year, when Brian Redman crashed his Porsche 908 32km (20 miles) or so into the first lap. The car caught fire, and Redman suffered extensive burns. It took 45 minutes for medical help to reach him, and the Porsche team did not know where he was for 12 hours. Eventually, teammates Pedro Rodríguez and Richard Attwood found him in a hospital in Cefalu.

Marko was racing on what was known as the *Piccolo* circuit. When the Targa Florio first started, in 1906, it covered three laps of a 92-mile lap that circumnavigated the whole island of Sicily. By the 1920s, the lap had been shortened to 108km (67 miles), and the event had become one of the most important races in Europe – it pre-dated both Le Mans and that other infamous Italian marathon road race, the Mille Miglia (see page 146). The Piccolo circuit was first used in 1932, after Benito Mussolini ordered the construction of a road connecting Caltavuturo and Collesano, two of the villages in the Madonie, and became the fixed layout from 1951.

The roll call of winners includes the most famous names of the pre-and post-war eras of racing. Tazio Nuvolari in 1931 and 1932, sandwiched by triumphs by his great rival Achille Varzi in 1930 and 1934. Luigi Villoresi won the last two events before World War II.

Stirling Moss and Peter Collins drove the winning Mercedes in 1955. In 1961, Ferrari F1 driver Wolfgang von Trips – killed at Monza later the same year when on the brink of the world title – shared the winning car with Belgian driver Olivier Gendebien.

Despite the efforts of Alfa Romeo and Ferrari, Porsche is the most successful manufacturer, with 11 wins. It meant so much to the company that they named a car after it – their hard-top convertible version of the 911 is called the Targa to this day.

OPPOSITE FAR RIGHT: The Ferrari Dino 206 of Ludovico Scarfiotti and Mike Parkes wrapped round a tree in 1966.

OPPOSITE RIGHT: In 1972 Arturo Merzario and Sandro Munari took their Ferrari 312 to a narrow victory over Helmut Marko and Giovanni 'Nanni' Galli. Their total time would never be bettered.

OPPOSITE BOTTOM: The Ferrari 250 GTO of Egidio Nicolosi in 1964.

BELOW: Helmut Marko giving it full gas on the mountain roads of Sicily in 1972 in his Alfa Romeo 33 TT3.

The lap took drivers from sea level up to well over 600m (1,969 ft) up in the mountains, and the topography and environment defined the event.

"One part is at the coast," Marko says, "you see the sea, Cefalu, quite a famous holiday resort. Then you go up in the mountains, and up there you don't see any buildings, or maybe a stone house. The asphalt is changing so much, and when it changes it has completely different grip. You are lonely in the mountains and you can hardly fit two cars in the road. When we were practising, there were a lot of accidents.

"And then you go through an agricultural area. There were goats, and some other animals and also during the race they were running around."

Cars were started at 15-second intervals because a full grid was not possible on the tight and twisty roads. Spectators stood several deep by the side of the road – and sometimes in it. During the race, residents of the villages inland would nail their front doors shut, lest they step outside at the same time as a car was racing past on the limit.

The race in 1972 devolved into a straight fight between Marko's Alfa, shared with Giovanni 'Nanni' Galli, and Merzario and his co-pilot Sandro Munari, soon to become synonymous with the Lancia Stratos in world rallying. By now, Marko had put his misgivings aside, and thrown caution to the wind. "We spent about three weeks practising," he says. "Then, I still had this approach: 'Okay, I have a contract, so I do this race.' But in the race, all of a sudden, I don't know what happened, but I was going fast.

"Part of why I got into race mode was the atmosphere, the people. They all were cheering. I don't know how they did the timekeeping but obviously they knew what was going on. You could hear: 'Forza, forza, forza.'

ABOVE AND OPPOSITE: Daniel Ricciardo felt even greater respect for his Red Bull motorsport director when he took Helmut's Alfa Romeo for a spin on the course in 2014.

TOP LEFT AND RIGHT: Unlike re-runs of the Mille Miglia, the Targa Florio has both classic recreations of the event with pre-1977 machinery (its final year of running outside the World Championship) and also Ferrari Owners' Club rallies with modern machinery.

"The Ferrari was the much better car and it was faster on the straight but I was catching. And I overtook the Ferrari twice on the road. I was following it for a while, no guardrails and 500,000 spectators. I said, 'Okay, I go (past) into the hairpin.' And the people moved. But if they hadn't moved...

"There were various dramas. Nanni Galli didn't have his best day. Twice I got into the lead and

he managed to lose the lead. Then he came for the last stop. He put the car so they couldn't change the tyres, and we lost I don't know how much. Then I caught up again and before the straight I was ahead. And after the straight, we lost by 12 seconds or so.

"I was driving, yeah, like mad, and sometimes it's just instinct when that came out. It was an unbelievable race. Unbelievable experience."

The Targa had just one more appearance as an internationally sanctioned race. In 1973, among many accidents, two were fatal. A spectator was killed, and seven others injured. That convinced the authorities that enough was enough, although it continued as a national event until 1977, when another accident that killed spectators brought down the curtain. These days, it survives in Sicily as a historic regularity rally, in which average speeds are defined, and there are spin-off events in Australia, New Zealand and Canada.

As for Marko, there was one more unique experience to come in Sicily in 1972. "You always had a party after the race," he says. "It was not 'first to the helicopter' like it is now." Marko was told that there was a 'gentleman' who wanted to see him. Marko demurred. He'd already had a fair bit of wine, and said he was having a nice time where he was. But then Chiti came over and said that there wasn't a choice.

"It was one man sitting," Marko says. "Next to him were two other guys. He of course didn't speak English. Some of his people translated: 'Very impressed — and you have a wish free.' I said: 'Fine, but I prefer to go back to my people.' So they gave me a card.

"The next day on the aeroplane, they came and said, 'What did he say, what happened?' It was the oldest mafia boss, and a 'wish free' means if I wanted to kill someone, he would have killed him. I never made use of it but at least I was threatening people with it."

Tour de Corse

Corsica, France

The Tour de Corse is one of the most evocative, and tragic, rallies in motorsport history – it has been the French round of the world championship from the inaugural season in 1973 until 2008, and again since 2015. It is famous for its twisty asphalt roads and beautiful mountain scenery on the Mediterranean island of Corsica – blue seas matching the blue skies that provide the backdrop for the famous white granite mountains.

Two-time world rally champion Carlos Sainz, who won in Corsica in 1991, says: "The stages are beautiful – very twisty, some new pieces of asphalt but also some very old and a mixture of sections: old, new, bumpy, fast, slow. It makes the rally very special.

"There are a few stages where there are big, big drops and it could be very challenging. Also the fact that you sometimes have stages as much as 45km (28 miles) long. It used to be long days with very long stages, the speed there is very high and I really enjoyed that rally. It was a very good challenge for everyone."

In Sainz's heyday, the Tour de Corse lived up to its name, it really was a tour of the entire island. Nowadays, with rallies shortened and made more compact, it focuses on the roads around the town of Ajaccio. But the character remains the same.

It is a rally typically won by a Frenchman. The two record holders are both French: six-time winners Bernard Darniche and Didier Auriol. Only four non-French drivers have won it more than once, all of them notable – legends Sandro Munari, Markku Alén and Colin McRae, and Thierry Neuville, who might not be a world champion like the others, but is a 19-time world rally winner, and ninth-equal in the all-time list with Markku Alén and Ott Tänak.

It is also a rally that will forever be associated both with tragedy and with rallying's peak era of popularity, the Group B era of the mid-1980s. In fact, two fatalities on successive years in 1985 and 1986 sealed the fate of Group B as they came to be seen as proof that the cars had become too fast and dangerous.

The first loss was Attilio Bettega. Driving his Lancia 037, the last remaining rear-wheel drive car to battle against the famous four-wheel drive Audi Quattros and Peugeot 205s, the Italian lost control and hit a tree on the fourth stage in 1985. His co-driver survived.

It was the death of Henri Toivonen the following year, however, that made the decisive impact. The Finn was the poster boy of the WRC and seen as the champion in waiting in 1986, driving the monster Lancia Delta S4 – the Italian company's answer to its German and French rivals.

Toivonen went off the road at a tight left-hand corner and rolled down a ravine. The car was destroyed in a fireball. There were no witnesses and all that remained of the car was its blackened spaceframe. Toivonen and his co-driver Sergio Cresta had no chance.

Within hours of the crash, the president of motorsport's governing body, Jean-Marie Balestre, banned Group B cars from the 1987 season, saying they were too dangerous.

OPPOSITE: The Red Bull and Shell-backed Hyundai of Dani Sordo on one of the coastal power stages in the 2019 Tour de Corse.

ABOVE: Toivonen and Cresta in the Lancia Delta S4 on the 1986 Tour de Corse. Toivonen, who was leading, had complained of exhaustion before his fatal crash.

Watkins Glen

New York, USA

Watkins Glen, a glorious high-speed road course in upper New York State, was the first real home of the United States Grand Prix. It's more than 40 years since 'the Glen' last hosted Formula 1, and the prospects of it ever doing so again are non-existent. But F1 driver Kevin Magnussen, who has competed in endurance racing there, reckons, "it would be amazing in these (modern) cars. So cool."

Now restricted to US racing, including an annual race of the country's biggest category, NASCAR stock cars, the 'long course' is still pretty much the same as it was back in the day. Magnussen describes the track as "like a mini-Green Hell, in a way", a reference to the Nürburgring Nordschleife. And compliments don't come much bigger for race tracks than that. "It's fast, flowing," Magnussen says. "There's not a lot of low-speed corners in Watkins Glen."

The honour of being first to host Formula 1 in the US goes to Sebring, a notoriously bumpy airfield circuit in Florida, which introduced the sport to America in 1959. Two years later, F1 switched to Watkins Glen, and it stayed there for 20 years.

Watkins Glen did not have the broad appeal of the US Grand Prix's latest home in Austin, Texas. Located out in the sticks at the southern tip of Seneca Lake, one of the area's glacial Finger Lakes, there were no fancy hotels, and fans tended to camp out.

The track hosted F1 five years after it was inaugurated, and its first grand prix was unusual for the absence of Ferrari. With the world title already sewn up, and mourning the death of Wolfgang von Trips in the Italian Grand Prix, Enzo Ferrari decided not to send his 156 'shark-nose' cars to America. He decision deprived the new world champion, Phil Hill, of the chance to celebrate his title at his home race.

Watkins Glen soon became one of the most popular events on the calendar with teams and drivers. This was long before the structured financial arrangements of modern F1, and the starting and prize money (the main form of income) at the US Grand Prix often exceeded that of the other races combined.

The track was the scene of stirring drives, and horrific tragedies. In 1970, Emerson Fittipaldi took his maiden victory for Lotus in only his fourth F1 start. It was the first race since their driver Jochen Rindt had been killed in a crash in practice at Monza, and the result guaranteed the Austrian would finish the year as F1's only posthumous world champion – Jacky Ickx's fourth place in his Ferrari ensured the Belgian could not score enough points at the final race in Canada to overhaul Rindt.

The following year was the first time F1 cars raced on the newly constructed long course, which extended the track from 3.78km (2.35 miles) to 5.42km (3.37 miles) with a newly added lower section.

It transformed the venue from a fast, short track, to a wooded one with extensive elevation, on which nearly every corner was banked and a rewarding challenge for drivers.

TOP: The charismatic François Cevert whose death hastened Jackie Stewart's retirement. Pierre Gasly wore a tribute helmet at the 2023 US Grand Prix (USGP), 50 years after the French driver's passing, a gesture much appreciated by Stewart.

ABOVE: Jackie Stewart (wearing sunglasses) in conversation with Jody Sheckter (right) during the 1973 race weekend.

OPPOSITE: Like Silverstone, the original Watkins Glen grid was on a bend. Ted Hopkins is about to start the 1965 race.

Tyrrell's François Cevert, Jackie Stewart's understudy, took his maiden victory that year. Stewart, the preeminent driver of the era, saw great promise in the glamorous Frenchman with stunning blue eyes, and spent the subsequent two years preparing him to take over as team leader.

Nevertheless, Cevert was unaware arriving at the 1973 race at Watkins Glen that Stewart planned to announce his retirement after what would be his 100th grand prix; indeed, Stewart had not even told his wife Helen, limiting the secret to team owner Ken Tyrrell and Ford's Walter Hayes.

But Cevert never got the chance to assume Stewart's mantle. In qualifying, he suffered a crash of sickening violence at the Esses. The impact lifted the barriers, which cut the driver in half. Colleagues who stopped at the scene of the accident were shellshocked. Stewart was one of them. Heartbroken, he retired on the spot.

The following year saw another horrendous accident, this time at Turn 7, known as Outer Loop, a long fast right-hander at the end of the back straight. The victim was 25-year-old Austrian Helmuth Koinigg, in only his second grand prix. Koinigg's Surtees suffered a suspension failure and he was pitched head-on at high speed into the barrier, which separated and decapitated him.

After these two accidents, a chicane was added before the Esses to slow the track down, and by the late 1970s its condition was deteriorating, along with its reputation. It was becoming notorious for rowdy fans, who, fuelled up with beer in the autumn chill, had taken to partying in a field that became known as 'the Bog'. Vandalism was common, including the torching of cars, and even once a Greyhound bus.

For its final two races, the Glen's fans witnessed something special. In 1979, Ferrari's Gilles Villeneuve burnished his growing reputation

as the fastest driver in the world with a performance in practice that has gone down in history. In teeming rain, only six cars went out. One who did was Villeneuve's teammate, the new world champion Jody Scheckter. He felt he'd driven well in the conditions, was sure he would be fastest. Only to return to the pits and see that Villeneuve had gone 9 seconds faster.

Villeneuve went on to qualify third, but in a race that started wet and finished dry, leapt into the lead at the start and dominated, for his third win of a year in which some saw him, not Scheckter, as the moral champion.

By now, the writing was on the wall for the track as an F1 venue. In 1980, organisers had needed a $750,000 loan from the Formula One Constructors' Association (FOCA) to pay prize money and other expenses – meaning the FOCA

BELOW LEFT: Patrick Head and Frank Williams with USGP East winner Alan Jones on what proved to be the Glen's final F1 race.

BELOW: Two mechanics, along with John Surtees, work on Helmuth Koinigg's car during practice at Watkins Glen in 1974.

BOTTOM: Jody Scheckter in the six-wheel Tyrrell P34 was only 8 seconds behind winner James Hunt in the 1976 race.

had essentially loaned the money that was then paid back to its members. When the debt was not repaid, and government funding was not forthcoming, the 1981 race was cancelled.

Now confined to US-based championships, the Glen's essential character remains. "It's like being in a movie scene," Magnussen says. "You know, sometimes you go to cities, like New York, and there is a special feeling because you're in a place

that you've seen so many times. I've seen and heard so much about the history of F1; it is great just to go there and be in the same spot on one of those tracks in a race car yourself.

"All the drivers stay in their motorhomes and barbecue in the night and it's that type of vibe still. That's what I really enjoy about US motorsport, the chilled out and laid-back approach to the sport."

ABOVE: Watkins Glen's major transformation came between the 1970 and 1971 seasons when the start line was moved back, ostensibly making the old final turn, the first turn on the new circuit. Today it hosts the major US series including the NASCAR Cup series pictured here.

Yas Marina Circuit

Yas Island, Abu Dhabi

At the inaugural race of the Yas Marina Circuit in 2009, Kimi Räikkönen was asked for his reaction to the new track. "Sector one is okay," he said. "The rest is a bit shit."

Diplomatic, it wasn't. At the time, Ferrari, for whom Räikkönen was racing, were sponsored by Abu Dhabi's sovereign wealth fund, and he was standing in a venue that was reputedly the most expensive Formula 1 circuit in history, built at an estimated cost of $1bn as a statement piece for the Gulf state's soft power. It certainly looked the part. The last section looped around a marina and past an impressive hotel dressed in a cover that was claimed to look like a whale, although some felt bore phallic resemblances, and festooned in LED lights that continuously changed colour in waves through the evening.

But Räikkönen spoke the truth. And in the years since that first race, there has been one overpowering question hanging over this glamorous but mundane race track. How, when money was no object, and with a blank canvas, could F1's favourite circuit architect Hermann Tilke have come up with something so dull?

The idea was good. Create a purpose-built race track on a man-made island, constructed solely for leisure purposes, and which now also features the Ferrari World theme park and an expansive water park. Several hotels within walking distance are arranged in a circle, with gardens behind, so that if you attended the race, you could stay just across the road, and have your pick of any number of restaurants, eating outside in the balmy temperatures. Or at least you could until the race grew in popularity and the prices became prohibitive.

But the track? A missed opportunity, to put it kindly. A couple of fast sweepers to start the lap, but then two long straights joined by a chicane and a succession of right-angled corners to finish, many of them off-camber, making it even harder to follow, keep tyres in good condition and overtake.

And while the inaugural race was uneventful, it was the second, at the end of 2010, that really laid bare the circuit's problems, during a four-way title showdown between Ferrari's Fernando Alonso, Red Bull drivers Mark Webber and Sebastian Vettel, and McLaren's Lewis Hamilton.

Alonso led on points going in, but his team bungled their strategy with an early pit stop and left the Spaniard stuck behind the Renault of Russian journeyman Vitaly Petrov. And this is where one of F1's best-ever racers remained for 27 laps, handing Vettel his first title and making all too clear how the circuit layout militated against overtaking, despite being theoretically devised to promote it.

The advent of the DRS overtaking aid the following year changed the face of F1 but Abu Dhabi continued to produce races defined more by tedium than action — a shame for a circuit that is contractually guaranteed to host the finale of every grand prix season.

The one time it did produce genuine drama was nothing to do with the circuit. In 2021, race director Michael Masi made up the rules as he went along at the climax of the bitter title battle between Max Verstappen and Lewis Hamilton, resulting in the destiny of the championship changing hands on the final lap.

In 2022, a tweak was made to the layout, replacing the sequence of right-angled corners after the second long straight with one, long, banked corner. It made little difference.

The event is popular among a certain section of fans who welcome the opportunity for some winter sun in an environment that's relaxed, as long as the local rules are followed. But they're not there for the excitement on track. Yas Marina remains what it has always been — a nice-looking missed opportunity of remarkable proportions.

OPPOSITE: Lewis Hamilton in action at Yas Marina in 2020.

BELOW: Kimi Räikkönen and Sebastian Vettel take a roller-coaster ride at Ferrari World, next door, in 2015.

Zandvoort

Zandvoort, Netherlands

The Dutch Grand Prix is a race about one man. It exists because of him and it would not exist without him. It was created to feed off the phenomenon of Max Verstappen, and the minute he leaves Formula 1, it will almost certainly go with him.

The seaside circuit in Zandvoort held world championship races from 1952 for more than 30 years with only the odd interruption. But it had fallen off the calendar after Niki Lauda took the final victory of his career by holding off McLaren teammate Alain Prost in 1985.

A lack of money, and difficulties with access, meant there was no obvious way for it to come back. Zandvoort held a prestigious annual Formula 3 race, the Masters (won over the years by both Verstappen and his father Jos), but that looked to be the end of its international motor racing possibilities.

Verstappen changed all that. His rapid rise in F1 was accompanied by crowds of thousands of Dutch spectators, most clad in orange, attending many races on the European continent. And in the Netherlands they saw an opportunity to cash in.

The result is effectively a four-day beachside party in honour of Verstappen. The grandstands are swamped in orange and smoke flares are constantly firing an orange fog across the circuit, while house music blasts out from early morning until after dark. The access problems caused by there being effectively only one road in and out of Zandvoort have been solved by basically banning driving. Spectators either stay in town and party non-stop, or catch the train to and from nearby Amsterdam and Harlem.

Verstappen is honoured and touched by the unquestioning admiration – though he is apparently unaffected by it, as he is by most things. Of the three races held since the track returned to the calendar in 2021, at the time of writing, he had won them all.

OPPOSITE AND BELOW LEFT: Two angles on Turn 1 at the 2023 Dutch Grand Prix, a race where 97% of the spectators are Max Verstappen fans.

BELOW: Renault drivers René Arnoux and Alain Prost lead the field through Turn 1, Tarzan, at the start of the 1982 race. Arnoux would have a massive shunt at the corner during the race when his throttle stuck open.

"It's just amazing that this is possible," he says. "I think nobody, like 10 years ago, even thought about a grand prix here. And that we're able to do that now is just fantastic and hopefully, of course, it will continue for a while. But for me, it's just amazing to be here, to see all the fans and drive such an incredible track."

The Zandvoort on which F1 races now is a shorter version of the original classic track, which arose as a result of World War II. The Nazi invaders built a straight road through the dunes on which to hold victory parades. Once the war was over, this was linked up with other roads that had been built to access coastal defensive positions to create an unquestionably great race track – both for racing and as a challenge to the drivers.

A long pit straight, entered from a fast right-hander, led into a banked hairpin, known as Tarzan, where overtaking was possible on both the inside and outside.

The circuit wound through the dunes to a banked hairpin known as Hugenholtzbocht, and where through the late 1970s and early 1980s photographers would gather for the chance to catch shots of Gilles Villeneuve's Ferrari doing the Canadian's trademark power slides.

Villeneuve was at the centre of one of the most iconic moments of Zandvoort's first period. He suffered a puncture and spun when battling for the lead with Alan Jones's Williams in 1979. Not one for half measures, Villeneuve then returned to the pits at unimaginable speed, his left rear tyre disintegrating as he went, and eventually tearing off the rear wheel and dragging showers of sparks behind him.

There were others, too. In 1967, Zandvoort was the location Lotus and Ford chose for the debut of the Cosworth DFV engine in the Lotus 49 chassis, thus starting one of the all-time great

car-engine combinations. Jim Clark won on its debut – and a new standard had been set for F1 engines. The Cosworth DFV was to keep winning for another 15 years, eventually taking more than 150 victories, before the turbo tide finally swept it away in the early 1980s.

Zandvoort was also the scene of one of the greatest tragedies of what have become known as F1's 'killer years'. In 1973, Roger Williamson crashed his March early in the race. He was uninjured but trapped in the upturned car, which then caught fire, as cars so often did back then. Fellow Briton David Purely stopped his car to try to rescue Williamson. But the race was allowed to continue and the marshals, lacking fireproof clothing, failed to help.

The television pictures of an increasingly desperate Purley trying in vain to rescue Williamson before eventually walking away, head hung low as he realises the awful truth, are harrowing in the extreme.

Once Zandvoort fell off the F1 calendar, the track was changed. To assuage concerns about noise pollution, the back part of the circuit was removed to ensure cars were further away from local residences.

The result was that while the first section, from Tarzan to the daunting downhill right-hander known as Scheivlak, Turn 7, was left the same, the track turned right soon after that into a new section of tighter corners, and the pit straight was shortened considerably. The overall length at just over 4.25km (2.64 miles) was more or less the same as before, and the driving challenge of Zandvoort remained, but the modifications made overtaking much more difficult.

The lack of run-off had been considered a major hindrance to any hopes of an F1 return, but once Verstappen's emergence added momentum, solutions were considered.

OPPOSITE: An aerial view of the track shows exactly how tight the circuit fits within its boundaries. Many thought that after Lauda's final victory in 1985, Zandvoort would never return to the F1 calendar.

TOP: Roger Williamson photographed in the pits before his second and final F1 race, the 1973 Dutch Grand Prix.

ABOVE: In 1979 Gilles Villeneuve makes it back to the Ferrari pit with his car's left-rear corner in tatters.

The result was to bank the Hugenholtz hairpin and last corner much more steeply, at 19 and 18 degrees.

The changes at Hugenholtz have had an especially interesting effect. The ideal racing line there is the opposite of what might be expected. No inside apexes here, the fastest way is to track right around the top of the corner, high on the banking, something first discovered by Fernando Alonso at the 2021 race, where despite driving a mid-grid Alpine, he was consistently the fastest driver through that corner.

And while that would suggest overtaking would become all but impossible there, Alonso (again) proved that wrong in 2023, when he discovered that there was actually quite a lot of grip low down on the banking, too, and used a dive down the hill to pass the cars of George Russell and Alex Albon on the first lap of the race.

He is one of many drivers to savour the unique atmosphere provided by the Dutch fans. "This is a very special race track," he says, "with all the fans and the energy going on, so you feel always very focused."

French Grand Prix / German Grand Prix

Paul Ricard/Hockenheim

France is the cradle of motorsport. The very first motor race with the title of 'grand prix' was the 1906 Grand Prix de l'Automobile Club de France held at Le Mans. Only the Italian Grand Prix has been held more times than the 90 of the French. And the sport's governing body is not only based in Paris, but is known by its French name: the Fédération Internationale de l'Automobile.

So it seems remarkable that, in the middle of the third decade of the 21st century, when Formula 1 is run by an American organisation that says it cherishes the sport's history, there is no French Grand Prix on the calendar — and yet there are

four in the Middle East, which held its first event only in 2004.

The reasons for this anomaly primarily come down to money, but it's not quite as simple as that. Wrapped into it are also factors such as location and even circuit design and availability. Essentially, France has ended up in the bizarre situation of not having a track that is regarded as appropriate or suitable to host a grand prix.

France has held grands prix on some magnificent tracks. Charade and Rouen were classic road circuits and extreme driving challenges, Reims

was famous for slipstreaming races on a triangular layout dominated by straights and hairpins. The Circuit de la Sarthe, which hosts the Le Mans 24 Hours, is high-speed and demanding and could make a marvellous location for F1.

Dijon-Prenois cascades up and down Burgundy hills and hosted perhaps the sport's most famous ever one-on-one battle between Gilles Villeneuve and René Arnoux in 1979. And Pau in south-west France is a fabulous street circuit that held F1 events until 1963 — the last won by Jim Clark — and still hosts Formula 3 races.

But only two circuits in the country hold the FIA Grade 1 licence required to host Formula 1 races — Paul Ricard in Provence and Magny-Cours in Nevers. These are the only two tracks that have hosted a grand prix since 1985. Dijon, which shared the French GP with Paul Ricard from 1974–1984, and Le Mans, are only Grade 2.

The issue with both Paul Ricard and Magny-Cours is that they are difficult to access and finding the required finances to hold a race has proved problematic. Ricard is only 32km (20 miles) from Toulon on the Côte d'Azur but it is on top of a hill with only one road in and out.

OPPOSITE: The coloured asphalt run-offs are wide at Paul Ricard with the blue and red stripes supposedly embedded with abrasives in the paint that scrub off speed.

LEFT: Maurício Gugelmin in the Leyton House March crashes into Nigel Mansell's Ferrari at the start of the 1989 race at Paul Ricard, an image that went global. The Brazilian was unhurt and took the restart from the pit lane.

Consequently, while there was widespread pleasure when the track returned a French GP to the calendar in 2018 after a ten-year absence, this soon turned into frustration at the poor access – traffic jams were notorious. Its contract was not renewed after it lapsed in 2022.

The fact that the track, built by the eponymous drinks magnate on pretty much the only flat piece of land in Provence, was of limited appeal and tended to produce soporific races – a reputation it developed through the 1970s and 1980s – hardly helped.

At Magny-Cours, the situation is difficult in a different way. Right in the heart of France, it is a two-and-a-half-hour drive south of Paris. The nearest town, Nevers, may be only 13km (8 miles) away, but it is a quiet rural place, and there are few hotels in the area.

Magny-Cours hosted the French Grand Prix from 1991 to 2008, but the deal initially came about through political connections to then-President François Mitterrand. When the political support fell away, so did the financial backing and therefore the race.

Nowadays, F1's owner Liberty Media is generally looking for state-of-the-art tracks that can host crowds of 100,000 annually on a sustainable basis near population centres – Austin, for example. Or for which the funding is guaranteed by a state looking for promotion – think Bahrain, Abu Dhabi and Qatar. Or street circuits in major cities, where, again, the funding is guaranteed.

TOP LEFT: The unmistakeable figure of Alfred Neubauer presiding over a Mercedes test at Hockenheim in 1954.

LEFT: Michael Schumacher celebrates winning his first German Grand Prix for Benetton in 1995 in front of an adoring Hockenheim crowd.

OPPOSITE: Despite the presence of Sebastian Vettel driving for Ferrari in 2016 and a Mercedes front row, there was a clear dip in attendance at the Hockenheim race.

France has no locations that fit those descriptions, so until a project is put together that does, it is unlikely to return to the calendar. The final added complication is that Monaco is a Francophone country which directly borders it, and it has become regarded as a proxy French event.

There is another major country in a similar position with a remarkable motorsport heritage, but no F1 race – Germany. Few nations have such a close relationship with motorsport, whether through major manufacturers such as Mercedes or Audi – both of whom will be in F1 by 2026 – or from the fact that only Italy, Monaco and Britain have held more grands prix. The first German Grand Prix was in 1926 – and only Italy hosted more races before World War II.

But Germany lost its place on the Formula 1 schedule in 2019 and the chances of it returning do not seem high. Like France, it has two Grade 1 circuits that could theoretically host a grand prix: Hockenheim and the Nürburgring (the modern track built in 1984, not the classic Nordschleife).

After the Nordschleife was deemed too dangerous following Niki Lauda's fiery accident in 1976, Hockenheim held the race from 1977 until 2006, the Nürburgring occasionally hosting an extra event usually called the European GP. From 2008, a deal was struck that would see the two tracks alternate the German Grand Prix. It lasted only until 2013, after which the Nürburgring hit financial trouble.

That left Hockenheim alone again, but the circuit organisers found it increasingly difficult to make the race pay beyond the Schumacher era and, since it fell off the calendar during Covid in 2020, it has not been possible to find a way back.

The pressure on the F1 calendar is ever-increasing. The sport finds itself caught in a conflict between a desire to hold more races and the increasing feeling that 2024's 24-race calendar is not sustainable on well-being grounds for those who work in the sport.

In those circumstances, it is hard to see a way back for France and Germany, however much the sport might want them.

Index

Picture Credits

Alamy: Pages 11, 12, 14, 15, 17, 20, 21, 25, 31, 36, 42 (left), 52, 54 (bottom), 55, 57 (top left), 57 (middle right), 64, 72 (left), 85 (top), 95 (top), 96 (bottom), 99 (bottom left and right), 100, 101, 102 (top), 103 (bottom), 107, 108, 110 (top right), 112, 113, 114, 115, 117 (top), 119 (top right), 120, 121 (top right), 125 (bottom), 126, 128, 129, 134 (top), 141, 146, 148 (top), 156, 157, 163 (bottom), 166 (left), 168, 169, 171, 173, 175 (bottom), 182, 183, 188 (top left), 189 (bottom right), 193, 198, 200, 202, 203, 207, 211, 217, 219, 221

Circuit de Charade: Page 71

Dreamstime: Page 154

Getty Images: Pages 4, 7, 16, 22, 26, 27, 40 (bottom), 53, 57 (top right), 57 (bottom right), 70, 73, 80, 83 (top right), 83 (bottom), 93, 94, 97, 98, 99 (top), 105, 106 (top), 107 (bottom), 118, 119 (top left), 121 (top left), 121 (bottom right), 127, 133, 137 (top), 138 (top), 147, 153, 158, 164, 172, 174, 194, 201, 218, 220 (bottom)

Grand Prix Photo.com: Pages 6, 9 (left), 10 (top), 23, 24, 28, 29, 30, 33, 34, 35, 37, 38, 39, 40 (top), 41, 42 (right), 43, 44, 45, 47 (top left), 47 (bottom), 48, 49, 50 (left), 51, 58 (right), 59, 60, 61, 62, 63, 65, 66, 67, 74, 75, 76, 77, 78, 79, 81,

82, 83 (left), 84, 85 (bottom), 86, 87, 88, 89, 90, 91, 102 (bottom), 103, 104, 109, 110 (top left), 110 (bottom right), 119 (bottom right), 122, 124, 132, 142, 143, 144, 145, 159, 160, 161, 162, 176, 177, 178, 181, 186, 187, 188 (top right), 189 (top), 189 (bottom left), 190, 191, 192, 194, 195, 196, 197, 208, 209, 210, 212, 213, 214, 215, 216, 220 (top)

Frank Hopkinson: Pages 184, 185

Library of Congress: Page 152

Porsche Motorsport: Pages 10 (bottom), 163 (top right)

Red Bull Content Pool: Pages 8, 54 (top), 123, 125 (top), 136, 137 (bottom), 138 (bottom), 139, 155, 166 (right), 175 (top), 179, 204 (bottom), 205, 206

Shutterstock: Pages 18, 19, 46, 47 (top right), 50 (top right), 50 (bottom right), 56, 58 (left), 68, 69, 95 (bottom), 96 (top), 111, 116, 130, 131, 134 (bottom), 135, 149, 150, 151, 170, 180, 204 (top left and right)

Volkswagen Motorsport: Pages 9 (right), 165, 167

Wikimedia Commons: Page 148 (bottom)